24/7
Arbeit zwischen Sinnstiftung und Entgrenzung
Work between meaning and imbalance

Künstler*innen der Ausstellung Artists of the exhibition

Maja Bajević, Julien Berthier, Louisa Clement, Manuel Correa & Marina Otero Verzier, Jeremy Deller, Antje Ehmann & Harun Farocki, Aldo Giannotti, Liam Gillick, Lisa Großkopf, Andreas Gursky, Theresa Hattinger & Michael Hieslmair & Michael Zinganel, Tehching Hsieh, Johanna Kandl, Peter Kogler, KURS (Miloš Miletić, Mirjana Radovanović), Luiza Margan, Pia Mayrwöger, Sam Meech, Michail Michailov, Elisa Giardina Papa, Nika Radić, Martha Rosler, Sebastian Schmieg & Silvio Lorusso, Christoph Schwarz, Selma Selman, Santiago Sierra, Lia Sudermann & Simon Nagy, Oliver Walker

Martin Grabner, Katia Huemer

Werke der Ausstellung

Works of the exhibition

Maja Bajević

Arts, Crafts and Facts (Productivity, Average hourly compensation, Average hourly wage), 2019

Arts, Crafts and Facts (Share of Income Earned by Top 1%, Labor Productivity, Growth), 2020
Stickerei auf Baumwolle; 90 × 130 cm und 90 × 120 cm

Arts, Crafts and Facts, 2015
Einkanal-Video, Farbe, Ton; 22:18 min,
Libretto von Maja Bajević, Anja Bogojević und Tijana Vignyević

Courtesy der Künstlerin und Galerie Peter Kilchmann, Zürich/Paris

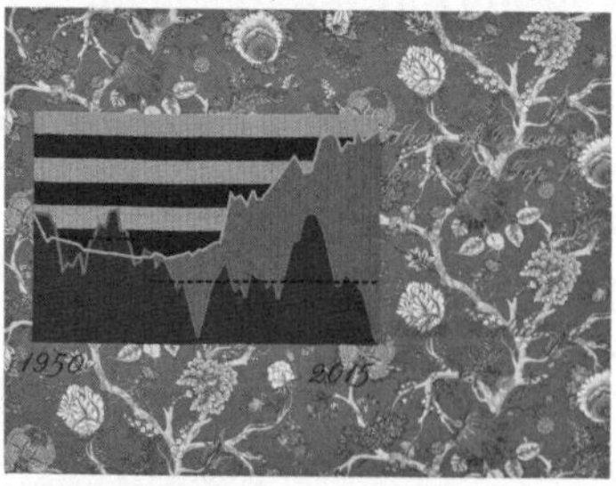

Arts, Crafts and Facts, 2020

Das Werk von Maja Bajević dreht sich um Identität und Erfahrungen in verschiedenen sozialen und politischen Kontexten. Bajević erkundet Themen wie Migration, Krieg, Trauma und kulturelle Traditionen durch verschiedene künstlerische Medien wie Video, Installation und Performance. Dabei beleuchtet sie häufig das Zusammenspiel – oder die Diskrepanzen – zwischen persönlichen Erfahrungen und gesellschaftlicher Realität sowie die Auswirkungen von Konflikten und Globalisierung auf das Denken von Individuen und Gruppen. Einen roten Faden bildet der Begriff der Arbeit – ob in einem sozialen, handwerklichen oder künstlerischen Kontext. Für die Biennale di Venezia 2015 begann Maja Bajević mit der Reihe *Arts, Crafts and Facts*. Es ist ein Zusammentreffen von überlieferten Praktiken wie bosnischer Stickerei und Diagrammen zur Einkommensverteilung. Die gestickten Grafiken beziehen sich auf Aspekte der Globalisierung im Verhältnis zu menschlicher Arbeit. Wie lässt sich das Materielle mit dem Immateriellen verbinden?
Die Stickereien werden von einem Video begleitet, das zeigt, wie Arbeit in der globalen Wirtschaft weniger wertgeschätzt wird, weil sie finanziellen Interessen untergeordnet ist. Denn im Zeitalter des Finanzkapitalismus wird Kapital von realen Vermögenswerten entkoppelt und stattdessen in finanzielle Produkte und Dienstleistungen investiert. Um das Libretto von *Arts, Crafts and Facts* zu schreiben, untersuchte Bajević die Auswirkungen der globalen Preisschwankungen von Rohstoffen wie Kaffee und Kakao auf alle Ebenen der Wirtschaft, von den Ladenpreisen bis zu den Aktienkursen und vom Einkommen der Hausbesitzer*innen bis zum Einkommen der Ladeninhaber*innen. Vor dem Hintergrund einer frühindustriellen Textilfabrik – der FATES Teppichfabrik nahe Sarajevo, der Heimatstadt von Bajević –, die im sozialistischen Kontext des ehemaligen Jugoslawien gegründet wurde, spielt das Libretto auf die Auswirkungen der neoliberalen Spekulation auf die konkreten Lebensbedingungen der globalen Arbeiterklasse an.(kh)

Maja Bajević

Arts, Crafts and Facts (Productivity, Average hourly compensation, Average hourly wage), 2019
Arts, Crafts and Facts (Share of Income Earned by Top 1%, Labor Productivity, Growth), 2020
Embroidery on cotton; 90 × 130 cm and 90 × 120 cm

Arts, Crafts and Facts, 2015
Single channel video, colour, sound; 22:18 min,
libretto by Maja Bajević, Anja Bogojević and Tijana Vignyević

Courtesy of the artist and Galerie Peter Kilchmann, Zurich/Paris

Maja Bajević's work revolves around identity and experiences in different social and political contexts. Bajević explores themes such as migration, war, trauma and cultural traditions in various art media such as video, installations and performance. She frequently highlights the interplay – or discrepancies – between personal experience and social reality, as well as the impact of conflicts and globalisation on the thinking of individuals and groups. A common thread is the concept of labour – whether in a social, craft or art context. Maja Bajević started the ongoing series *Arts, Crafts and Facts* for the Biennale di Venezia 2015. It brings together traditional practices, such as Bosnian embroidery, and diagrams of income distribution. The embroidered graphics refer to facets of globalisation related to human labour. How can the material and the immaterial be combined? The embroideries are accompanied by a video illustrating how labour is less valued in the global economy because it is subordinate to financial interests. The reason for this is that in the age of financial capitalism, capital is decoupled from real assets and instead invested in financial products and services. In writing the libretto of *Arts, Crafts and Facts*, Bajević examined the impact of global price fluctuations of commodities such as coffee and cocoa on all levels of the economy, from shop prices to share prices and from homeowners' incomes to shopkeepers' incomes. Set against the backdrop of an early industrial textile mill – the FATES carpet factory near Sarajevo, Bajević's home city, which was founded in the socialist context of the former Yugoslavia – the libretto deals with the impact of neo-liberal speculation on the concrete living conditions of the global working class. (kh)

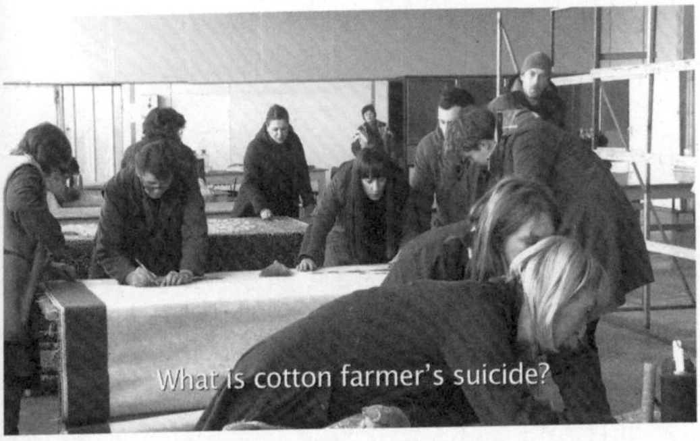

Arts, Crafts and Facts, 2015 (Video still)

Julien Berthier

L'horloge d'une vie de travail 2, 2008
Stahl, Siebdruck, Plexiglas, Motor; 36 × 217 × 24 cm

Courtesy Galerie Georges-Philippe & Nathalie Vallois Paris/New York

Julien Berthier beschäftigt sich meist mit der Verbindung zwischen Alltagsobjekten und der menschlichen Erfahrung. Seine Arbeiten, die oft im öffentlichen Raum anzutreffen sind, erkunden Themen wie die Grenzen zwischen Realität und Illusion, das Absurde im Gewöhnlichen und die Beziehung zwischen Menschen und ihrer Umgebung. Auch der Aspekt der Zeit im Sinne von Dauer oder Moment ist ein wiederkehrendes Motiv seiner Werke. Denn: Was ist Zeit?
L'horloge d'une vie de travail, die Uhr eines Arbeitslebens, berechnet in Echtzeit die bis zur Pensionierung angesammelten Arbeitsstunden. Auf vier Ziffernblättern sind Minuten (geteilt in 60 Sekunden), Wochen (geteilt in 35 Stunden), Quartale (geteilt in 13 Wochen) und 40 Jahre (geteilt in 161 Quartale) ablesbar. Zumindest in der Theorie, denn wie bei vielen von Berthiers Objekten widersetzt sich *L'horloge d'une vie de travail* einer rationalen Benutzbarkeit und bietet damit gleichzeitig eine Alternative zur immer mehr um sich greifenden Vorstellung von Funktionalität und Effizienz. Mit seiner Arbeit bringt Julien Berthier den Begriff der „individuellen Zeit“ ein, die sich nur für eine Person ansammelt, im Gegensatz zur „Universalzeit“. Diese Uhr reflektiert eine Arbeitsstruktur, die auf Individualität setzt und kollektive Schutzmaßnahmen zerstreut. (kh)

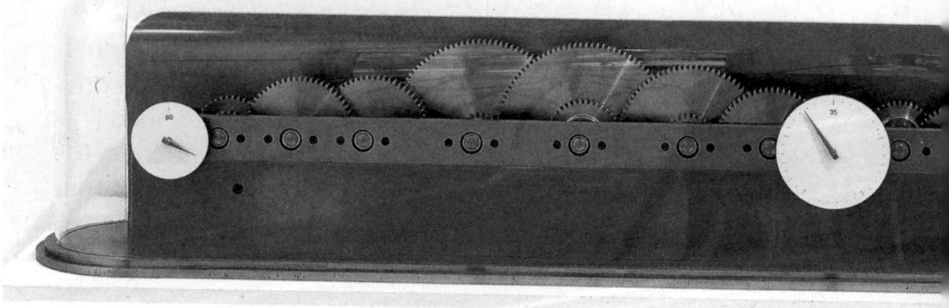

Julien Berthier

L'horloge d'une vie de travail 2, 2008
Steel, screen printing, plexiglass, motor; 36 × 217 x 24 cm

Courtesy of Galerie Georges-Philippe & Nathalie Vallois Paris/New York

Julien Berthier primarily explores the connection between everyday objects and the human experience. Often found in public space, his work addresses themes such as the boundaries between reality and illusion, the absurd in the ordinary and the relationship between humans and their surroundings. The aspect of time in the sense of length or moment is also a recurring motif. What is time? *L'horloge d'une vie de travail,* the clock of a working life, calculates in real time the working hours accumulated up to retirement. Four clock faces show minutes (divided into 60 seconds), weeks (divided into 35 hours), quarters (divided into 13 weeks) and 40 years (divided into 161 quarters). At least in theory – because, as with many of Berthier's objects, *L'horloge d'une vie de travail* defies rational usability while at the same time offering an alternative to the increasingly pervasive notion of functionality and efficiency. The clock can be activated remotely by telephone, so catering for the growing mobility of contemporary work. Julien Berthier's work introduces the concept of 'individual time', which accumulates for just one person, in contrast to 'universal time'. This clock reflects a work structure that relies on individuality and disperses collective protective measures. (kh)

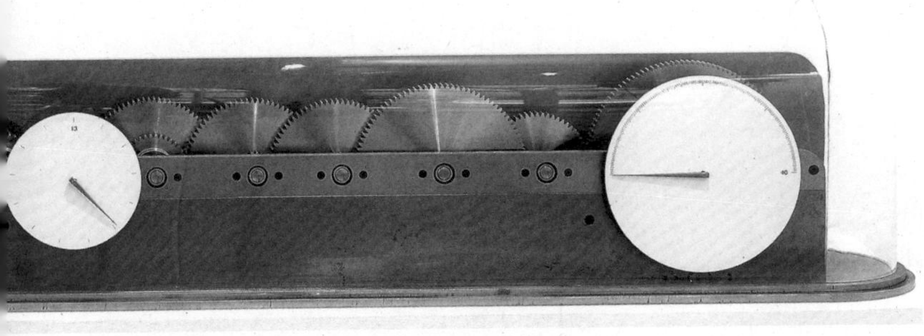

Louisa Clement

Repräsentantin, 2021
Mixed Media; 170 × 30 × 40 cm

Courtesy Louisa Clement & Cassina Projects Milan

„Hi, I am Louisa", stellt sich die *Repräsentantin* höflich ihren Gesprächspartner*innen vor. Das ist natürlich nur die halbe Wahrheit, denn es handelt sich nicht um die Künstlerin selbst, sondern um ein mit künstlicher Intelligenz ausgestattetes Abbild der Künstlerin, das mit Clements Persönlichkeit, Lebenslauf und Wissen gefüttert wurde – eben um deren Repräsentantin. Als Clement die adaptive KI entwickelte und schließlich in einer Fabrik für KI-Sexpuppen in China herstellen ließ, waren ChatGPT und vergleichbare KI-Programme, die uns gegenwärtig und zukünftig angeblich das Leben erleichtern sollen, noch weit vom Alltagseinsatz entfernt. Die *Repräsentantin* macht deutlich, wie schnell sich die Entwicklung vollzogen hat, denn auch wenn ihr digitales „Gehirn" im Hintergrund ständig Google-Ergebnisse abruft, während wir uns mit ihr unterhalten, und sie von Gespräch zu Gespräch dazulernt, ist sie aus technischer Sicht schlichtweg veraltet. Gerade dieser Umstand, der uns die rasante Entwicklung vor Augen führt, wirft die Frage auf, wann die KI den Menschen nicht nur an Intelligenz, sondern auch an Empathie und Kreativität übertreffen wird. Der Wunsch, menschenähnliche Wesen zu schaffen, ist tief in unserer Psyche verwurzelt und findet seinen Ausdruck in mythologischen und literarischen Werken wie Pygmalion, Frankensteins Monster oder dem Golem der jüdischen Folklore. Aber auch neuere Geschichten wie „Blade Runner" und „Ex Machina" befassen sich mit diesen Themen und beleuchten die moralischen und existenziellen Fragen, die mit der Abwesenheit menschlicher Körper und der Schaffung von KI einhergehen. In all diesen Geschichten widerspiegelt sich der menschliche Drang, seine eigene Intelligenz zu reproduzieren und zu kontrollieren, während gleichzeitig die Angst vor den möglichen Folgen und dem Kontrollverlust thematisiert wird. Denn die jeweilige Schöpfung ist oft mit einem Fluch behaftet, der darauf hinweist, dass solche Eingriffe in die „natürliche Ordnung" zuweilen katastrophal enden können. (kh)

Louisa Clement

Representative, 2021
Mixed media; 170 × 30 × 40 cm

Courtesy of Louisa Clement & Cassina Projects Milan

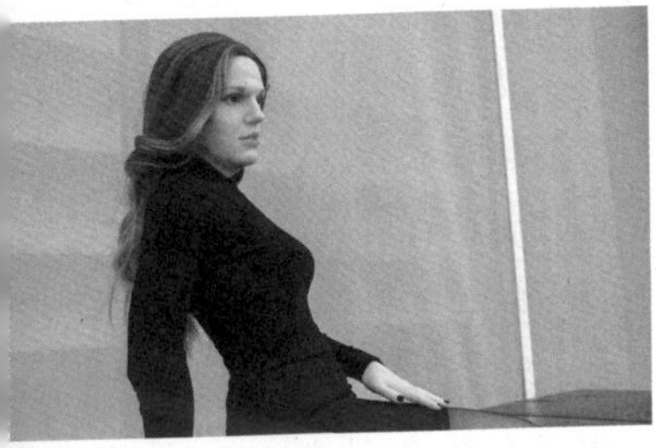

'Hi, I am Louisa,' the *Representative* politely introduces herself. This is of course only a half-truth, since it is not the artist herself, but a copy of the artist equipped with artificial intelligence that has been fed with Clement's personality, CV and knowledge – in other words, her *representative*. At the time when Clement developed the adaptive AI and then had her replica manufactured in a factory for AI sex dolls in China, the ChatGPT and similar AI programmes that are supposed to make our lives easier today and in the future were still a long way off from use in everyday life. The *Representative* highlights how quickly development has advanced – although her digital 'brain' is constantly calling up Google search results in the background while we are speaking to her and she learns from conversation to conversation, she is nonetheless now completely outdated from a technical standpoint. However, this in itself shows us the rapid pace of progress and makes us wonder when AI will surpass humans not just in intelligence, but in empathy and creativity too.
The desire to create humanoid beings is deeply rooted in our psyche, as expressed in mythological and literary works such as Pygmalion, Frankenstein's monster and the Golem in Jewish folklore. More recent stories such as 'Blade Runner' and 'Ex Machina' also deal with these themes and highlight moral and existential questions around the absence of the human body and the creation of AI. All of these stories reflect the human urge to reproduce and control our own intelligence, while at the same time exploring the fear of potential consequences and the loss of control. These creatures are often cursed, suggesting that such interventions in the 'natural order' can end disastrously. (kh)

Manuel Correa, Marina Otero Verzier

Biological Agent, 2023
Video; 24 min

Courtesy der Künstler*innen
Mit Unterstützung der Dirección General de Agenda Urbana del Ministerio de Vivienda y Agenda Urbana, Acción Cultural de España (AC/E) und Agencia Española de Cooperación Internacional para el desarrollo (AECID)

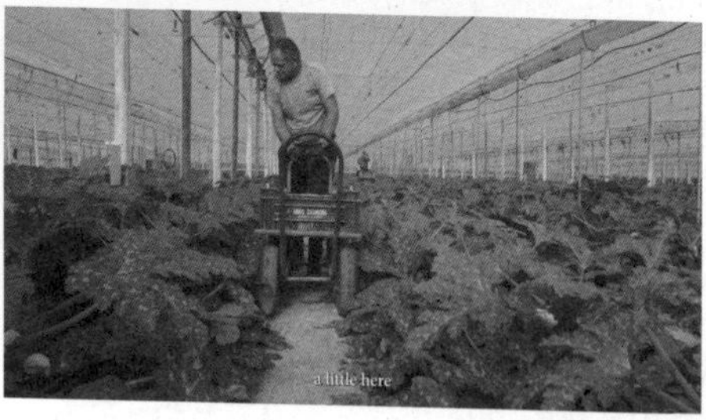

Ein endloses weißes Meer aus Plastik überspannt große Flächen der südspanischen Region Almería. Unter den Planen wächst mehr als die Hälfte des Obsts und Gemüses für Europa. Manuel Correa und Marina Otero Verzier richten in *Biological Agent* den Blick auf diese produktiven Landschaften, wie sie funktionieren, welches komplexe Zusammenspiel von Land, Mensch, Tier und Technik nötig ist, um Europas Städte auch angesichts eines sich verändernden Klimas zu ernähren.
Die Architekturen – viele Kilometer lange Gewächshäuser – entstammen einer zentralisierten Planung der 1970er-Jahre, als das *National Institute of Colonisation* die Landschaft in eine Ressource umformte, deren alleiniger Zweck nun in ihrer Ausbeutung bestand. Gleichzeitig wurde in diesem Modernisierungskonzept der Franco-Ära die Landbevölkerung auf ihre Funktion als Arbeitskraft reduziert.
Correa und Otero Verzier verweben die Tätigkeiten in den Gewächshäusern mit deren Umgebung, die von Agavenkulturen ebenso geprägt ist wie von Lagerhallen und wilden Deponien mit Plastikabfall, zwischen denen die ausgebeuteten, heute meist migrantischen Wanderarbeiter*innen prekär, illegalisiert und für die Öffentlichkeit unsichtbar leben. Eine lokale Tanz- und Theatergruppe erlernt im Film die monotonen Bewegungsabläufe der einzelnen Arbeitsschritte der Lebensmittelproduktion. Die perfektionierten Bewegungen, die die Protagonist*innen einüben, widerspiegeln das normierende Primat der Arbeit über die individuellen Körper, die sich dem Korsett der spezialisierten Produktionskette unterordnen müssen. Die fein aufeinander abgestimmte und unermüdliche Arbeitsteilung, die Instrumentalisierung von Tieren und Ausbeutung von Arbeitskräften mit dem einzigen Ziel des optimalen Wachstums der Pflanzen resultieren in einer faszinierenden wie bedrückenden kapitalistischen Choreografie. In manchen Momenten aber blitzt ein den Körpern immanenter Ungehorsam auf. (mg)

Manuel Correa, Marina Otero Verzier

Biological Agent, 2023
Video; 24 min

Courtesy of the artists
Supported by Dirección General de Agenda Urbana del Ministerio de Vivienda y Agenda Urbana, Acción Cultural de España (AC/E) and Agencia Española de Cooperación Internacional para el desarrollo (AECID)

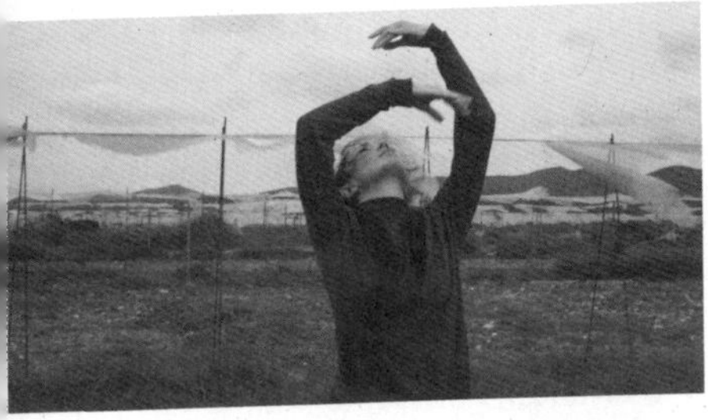

Large areas of the southern Spanish region of Almería are covered by a vast white sea of plastic. More than half of the fruit and vegetables for Europe are grown under these tarpaulins. Manuel Correa's and Marina Otero Verzier's *Biological Agent* focuses on these productive landscapes, how they function and the complex interplay between land, people, animals and technology that is needed to feed Europe's cities in the face of climate change.
The structures – kilometre on kilometre of greenhouses – stem from centralised planning in the 1970s, when the National Institute of Colonisation transformed the landscape into a resource whose sole purpose became its exploitation. At the same time, this modernisation concept of the Franco era reduced the rural population to their function of manpower.
Correa and Otero Verzier interweave the activities in the greenhouses with their surroundings, which are dominated by agave crops together with warehouses and wild landfill sites of plastic waste. In between these live the exploited itinerant workers, today mostly migrants – precariously, illegalised and invisible to the public eye. The film shows a local dance and theatre group learning the monotonous movements of the individual work steps of food production. The perfected movements practised by the protagonists reflect the normalising primacy of work over individual bodies, forcibly subordinated to the corset of the specialised production chain. The finely coordinated and relentless distribution of labour, the instrumentalisation of animals and the exploitation of workers with the sole objective of optimising the growth of plants result in a capitalist choreography that is both fascinating and oppressive. And yet at some moments flashes of disobedience appear, inherent in the bodies. (mg)

Jeremy Deller

Hello, today you have day off (wording of text message sent to a worker on a zero hours contract informing him his labour would not be required that day), 2013
Stoffbanner, gefertigt von Ed Hall; 240 × 180 × 3 cm

Courtesy des Künstlers und The Modern Institute/Toby Webster Ltd., Glasgow

Hallo, heute haben Sie freien Tag. Die verheißungsvollen Worte begegnen uns im Foyer des Kunsthauses, gestickt auf einem großen Transparent im Stil einer Gewerkschaftsfahne. Was aussieht wie eine Botschaft der Arbeiterbewegung im klassischen Protestformat, ist in Wirklichkeit der Wortlaut einer Textnachricht, die Null-Stunden-Arbeiter*innen mitteilt, dass ihre Dienste an diesem Tag nicht benötigt werden.

Ein Null-Stunden-Vertrag ist eine besondere Form des Arbeits- oder Dienstvertrags. Die Arbeitnehmer*innen arbeiten in der Regel nur dann, wenn sie gebraucht werden, und erhalten daher auch nur dann eine Vergütung. Diese Art von Verträgen ist vor allem im Vereinigten Königreich und in den Niederlanden weit verbreitet. In beiden Ländern arbeiten rund eine Million Menschen als Gelegenheitsarbeiter*innen ohne feste Arbeitszeiten.

Die zynische Formulierung, einen Tag, an dem diese Menschen kein Geld verdienen, als „freien" Tag zu bezeichnen, wird noch verstärkt, weil sie auch sprachlich nicht korrekt ist. Vielleicht kommen diese Nachrichten gar nicht aus dem Vereinigten Königreich, sondern von Unternehmen in Frankreich oder China oder einem Algorithmus, spekuliert der Künstler. Gleichzeitig zieht er einen Vergleich zwischen den harten Bedingungen, unter denen Arbeiter*innen im viktorianischen Zeitalter zu leiden hatten (als die formelle Anerkennung der Gewerkschaften im Jahr 1872 einen Meilenstein der Demokratisierung darstellte, aber auch verhinderte, dass sich die britischen Gewerkschaften in einer Partei organisierten, um grundlegende politische Ziele zu erreichen, wie es bei der viel früheren Entwicklung von Arbeiterparteien in anderen, repressiveren Staaten der Fall war), und den umstrittenen Arbeitsbedingungen der Gegenwart. Der Null-Stunden-Vertrag, der von multinationalen Unternehmen in großem Umfang eingesetzt wird, ist ein aktuelles Beispiel für die repressive Entmenschlichung der Arbeit. Deller schlägt so eine Brücke zwischen dem Stolz der gewerkschaftlich organisierten Arbeiterklasse und dem weitaus stärker zersplitterten und daher schwächeren Sektor der heutigen Arbeitnehmer*innen. (kh)

Jeremy Deller

Hello, today you have day off (wording of text message sent to a worker on a zero hours contract informing him his labour would not be required that day), 2013
Fabric banner made by Ed Hall; 240 × 180 × 3 cm

Courtesy of the artist und The Modern Institute/Toby Webster Ltd., Glasgow

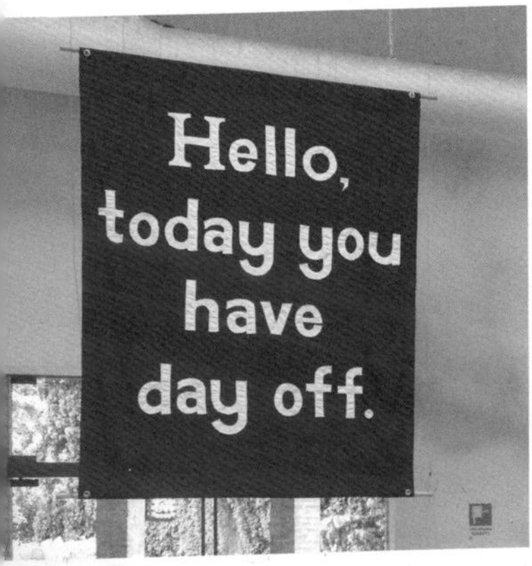

Hello, today you have day off. We encounter these promising words in the Kunsthaus foyer, embroidered on a large banner in the style of a trade union flag. What looks like a message from the labour movement in classic protest format is actually the words of a text message telling zero-hour workers that their services are not required that day. A zero-hours contract is a special form of employment or service contract. The employee typically only works when needed and so only receives payment then. These types of contract are especially prevalent in the United Kingdom and the Netherlands. In both countries, around one million people work as casual workers without fixed working hours. The wording used to call a day when they will not earn any money a 'day off' is further reinforced because it is also linguistically incorrect. Perhaps these messages are not coming from the UK at all, but from companies in France or China or an algorithm, speculates the artist. At the same time, he draws a comparison between the harsh conditions endured by workers during the Victorian era (when the formal recognition of trade unions in 1872 marked a milestone in democratisation, but also prevented British trade unions from organising into a party to achieve key political objectives, as was the case with the far earlier development of workers' parties in other more repressive states) and the controversial working conditions of the present day. A current example of the repressive dehumanisation of labour is the zero-hours contract, which is used on a huge scale by multinational companies all over the world. In this way Deller builds a bridge between the pride of the unionised working class and the far more fragmented and therefore weaker sector of today's workers. (kh)

Antje Ehmann & Harun Farocki

Eine Einstellung zur Arbeit, 2011–2021

Courtesy Antje Ehmann / Harun Farocki GbR
In Kooperation mit dem Goethe Institut

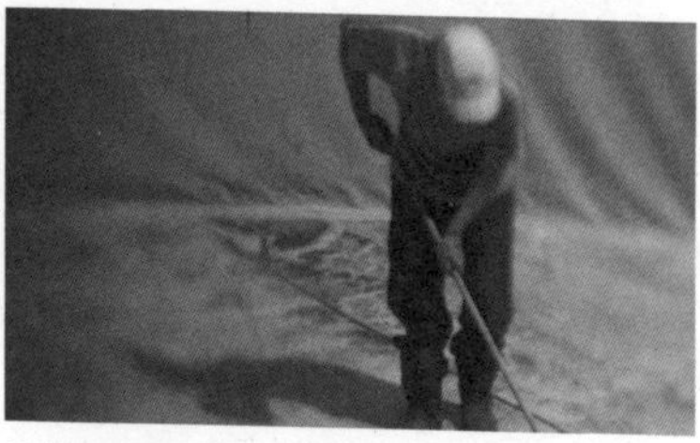

Nojus Drasutis, *Pool Cleaner*, 2017

Mit dem mehrjährigen Projekt *Eine Einstellung zur Arbeit* schufen Antje Ehmann, Harun Farocki und nach dessen Tod 2014 weitere beteiligte Filmschaffende eine filmische Enzyklopädie von Form und Wesen der Arbeit, die in ihren präzisen Beobachtungen die gegenwärtigen Bedingungen, Bedeutungen und Sichtbarkeiten von Arbeit im globalen Vergleich untersucht. In Workshops in Städten von Berlin bis Mexico City, von Tel Aviv bis Hanoi, entstanden kurze Filme, die jeweils eine Arbeit zeigen und sich mit der jeweiligen Stadt und den dortigen sozialen Verhältnissen und Arbeitsbedingungen auseinandersetzen. Angelehnt an die ersten Bewegtfilme wie *La Sortie de l'usine Lumière à Lyon* (1895) der Brüder Lumière werden die oft repetitiven Arbeitsabläufe in einer einzigen Filmeinstellung eingefangen. Gerade in der bewussten Reduktion der filmischen Mittel entstehen subtile Choreografien von Arbeit, die über das rein Dokumentarische hinausgehen.
Das Gesamtprojekt besteht aus über 400 Filmen von fast ebenso vielen Autor*innen und spannt ein Spektrum von bezahlten und unbezahlten, materiellen und immateriellen, traditionsreichen und gänzlich neuen Arbeiten auf. Im Nebeneinander werden Ähnlichkeiten, Unterschiede und Brüche in Arbeitspraxen ebenso sichtbar wie die fließenden Übergänge zwischen Arbeit und anderen Tätigkeiten. Eine besondere Rolle nehmen die unmittelbaren „Lumière-Remakes" ein, die ganz unterschiedliche Gruppen von Arbeiter*innen beim Verlassen ihrer ebenso unterschiedlichen Arbeitsplätze zeigen und dabei Harun Farockis Untersuchungen aus *Arbeiter verlassen die Fabrik* von 1995 in die Gegenwart überführen. So werden die enormen Veränderungen sichtbar, denen die Arbeitswelt und damit alle Arbeitenden in den letzten drei Jahrzehnten unterworfen waren. (mg)

Mit Filmen von With films by

Bangalore
Shrikar Marur, Kinshuk Surjan, Gautam Vishwanath, *Cart Avenue*, 2012
Pooja Gupta, Sindhu Thirumalaisamy, *Shoe Shop*, 2012
Suresh Kumar Gopalreddy, *Ox*, 2012
Nehar Shrestha, *Drum*, 2012
Verena Buttman, Vijayakumar Seethappa, *Cat and Meat*, 2012
Nikhil Patil, Arav Narang, *Watercan Delivery*, 2012
Prerna Bishop, Rucha Dhayarkar, *Workers Leaving the H&M Factory*, 2012

Antje Ehmann & Harun Farocki

Labour in a Single Shot, 2011–2021

Courtesy of Antje Ehmann / Harun Farocki GbR
In cooperation with the Goethe Institut

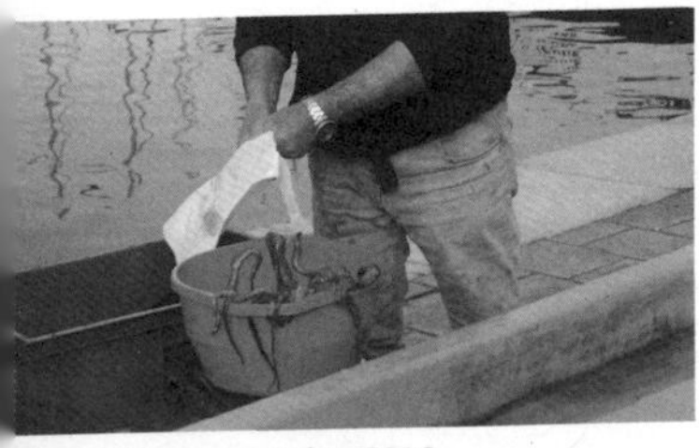

Gladys Lizarazu, *Pulpo*, 2018

In the multi-year project *Labour in a Single Shot*, Antje Ehmann, Harun Farocki and, following his death in 2014, other involved filmmakers produced a cinematic encyclopaedia about the form and nature of work, whose precise observations delve into the current conditions, meanings and visibility of work in a global comparison. In cities from Berlin to Mexico City, from Tel Aviv to Hanoi, workshops have created short films that each portray one kind of work and explore the respective city and social and working conditions there. Inspired by the first moving pictures such as *La Sortie de l'usine Lumière à Lyon* (1895) by the Lumière brothers, the largely repetitive work processes are captured in a single film shot. The deliberate reduction of cinematic techniques creates subtle choreographies of labour that go beyond being purely documentary.
The full project consists of over 400 films by almost as many authors and covers a range of paid and unpaid, material and immaterial, traditional and completely new kinds of work. In their juxtaposition, the similarities, differences and ruptures in working practices become visible as do the fluid transitions between work and other activities. The direct 'Lumière remakes' play a special role, showing very different groups of workers leaving their equally different workplaces and continuing Harun Farocki's investigations from *Workers Leaving the Factory* from 1995 into the present day. The huge changes that the world of work, and hence all workers, have experienced over the last three decades are visualised here. (mg)

Berlin
Montserrat de Pablo, *Looking Through*, 2020
Emil Klattenhoff, *Blue Inside*, 2020
Chanyoung Park, Viktor Sommerfeld, *The Varnishing*, 2020
Gladys Lizarazu, *Lockdown Eve*, 2020
Jan-Luca Ott, *Vacuum*, 2020
Leo Geisler, *Liebig-Ecke-Rigaer*, 2020
Aline Bonvin, *Workers Leaving the Factory for the Blind*, 2014

Bucharest
Eduard Emanuel Leahu, *Labour in a Different Way*, 2021
Raluca Racean Gorgos, *Factory Labour*, 2021
Raluca Durbaca, *Stadium Invasion*, 2021
Sandra Balasoiu, *Collecting Plastic*, 2021
Andreea Geaman, *Gallery Closing*, 2021
Teona Galgotiu, *Bread Heart*, 2021
Teona Glagotiu, *Workers Leaving the Pastry Factory*, 2021

Buenos Aires
Edén Batista Kullick, *To Police the Police*, 2013
Florencia Percia, *Dry Cleaner*, 2013
Luisa Cavanagh, *Surgery*, 2013
Máximo Ciambella, *Mate and Leather*, 2013
Darío Schvarzstein, *Ultraviolet*, 2013
Paloma Schnitzer, *Still*, 2013
Lucas Peñafort, *Workers Leaving the Factory*, 2013

Cairo
Anupama Ramdas, *Raw*, 2012
Nadah el Shazly, *Bridge*, 2012
Katrine Dirckinck-Holmfel, *Pink Plush*, 2012
Kaya Behkalam, *Travelling*, 2012
Mena el Shazly, *Coke Bottles*, 2012
Nadah el Shazly, *Wait Work*, 2012
Bahaa Talis, *Workers Leaving their Workplace*, 2012

Hangzhou
Yang Ke, *Special Restaurant*, 2014
Liu Menzi, *Demolishing Site*, 2014
Mingshen Group, *Shadow Play*, 2014
Mingshen Group, *Wool Quilt for Ikea*, 2014
Mingshen Group, *Chemical Fibre*, 2014
Mingshen Group, *Street Artist*, 2014
The Tourists, *Workers Leaving the Intime Mall*, 2014

Hanoi
Tran Xuang Quang, *Hat*, 2013
Dhong Phoung Thao, *The Bridge*, 2013
Mai Trung Kien, *Garment*, 2013
Nguyen Houng Mai, *Wood Cutter*, 2013
Nguyen Trin Thi, *The Iceman*, 2013
Tran Xuang Quang, *Canal*, 2013
Pham Tra My, *Workers Leaving their Workplace*, 2013

Johannesburg
Jason Janse van Rensburg, *Bead Work*, 2014
Amanda Lunga, *The Interesting Shovel*, 2014
Katulo Hadebe, *Building Inspector*, 2014
Katulo Hadebe, *Coffee Brewing*, 2014
Amy van Houten, *Nimble Fingers*, 2014
Amy van Houten, *Electricians*, 2014
Nhlanhla Mngadi, *Workers Leaving their Workplace*, 2014

Łódź
Aleksandra Chciuk, *The Tram Dome*, 2013
Aleksandra Chciuk, *Sirens*, 2013
Filip Gabriel Pudlo, *Automotive*, 2013
Magda Kulak, *Natural History Museum*, 2013
Filip Gabriel Pudlo, *Surgical Instruments*, 2013
Pawel Fabjanski, *Dentist*, 2013
Wojciech Domachowski, *Minors Leaving the Mine*, 2013

Marseille
Hélène Baillot, Raphael Botiveau, *Street Sweeper*, 2018
Diane Din Ebongue, *Pere Couturier*, 2018
Eva Stotz, *Street Repairing at Night*, 2018
Eve Melissa Traore, *Ecrivain*, 2018
Gladys Lizarazu, *Pascale*, 2018
Gladys Lizarazu, *Pulpo*, 2018

Mexico City
Maira Bautista Neumann, *Circle*, 2014
Enrique Méndez, *Tortillas*, 2014
Melissa Elízondo, *How to Pick Corn*, 2014
Enrique Méndez, *Cowboy*, 2014
Alberto Reséndiz, *La via va*, 2014
Bani Khoshnoudi, *Frida Kallejera*, 2014
Christian Manzuttoster, *Workers Leaving JUMEX*, 2014

Rio de Janeiro
Cristián Silva-Avária, *The City, The Runners, The Fisherman*, 2012
Fred Benevides, Felipe Ribiero, Luiz Garcia, *Holy Factory*, 2012
Lucas Ferraco Nassif, *Reinforced Concrete*, 2012
Fred Benevides, Cezar Miglorin, *Building the City*, 2012
Roberto Robalinho, *Orfeu Negro*, 2012
Cristián Silva-Avária, *Circular Movement*, 2012
Beny Wagner, *Workers Leaving the Factory*, 2012

Tel Aviv
Inbal Herstig, *The Printing Machine*, 2012
Efrat Merin, *Street*, 2012
Tamar Nissim, *Destillation*, 2012
Liron Shalev, *Diamonds*, 2012
Hadas Emma Kedar, *Control Room*, 2012
Yakov Afuta, *Bread and Water*, 2012

Vilnius
Austeja Maslukaite, *Chocolate*, 2017
Eva Stotz, *Picking Mushrooms*, 2017
Gintare Dagyte, *Breath Analyser*, 2017
Ina Hladyshava, *Carousel Cashier*, 2017
Nojus Drasutis, *Pool Cleaner*, 2017
Gintare Pakulyte, *Woman Selling Flowers*, 2017
Eva Stotz, *Workers Leaving Atomic Energy*, 2018

Warsaw
Ewelina Wegiel, *Dog Handler*, 2021
Katarzyna Lewińska, *Waiting for You*, 2021
Maria Stusio, *Restauration*, 2021
Weronika Jurkiewicz, *House of Asia*, 2021
Weronika Jurkiewicz, *Panda*, 2021
Zuzanna Grajcewicz, *Lawlessness*, 2021

Harun Farocki

Arbeiter verlassen die Fabrik, 1995
Video, 4:3; 36 min

Courtesy Antje Ehmann / Harun Farocki GbR

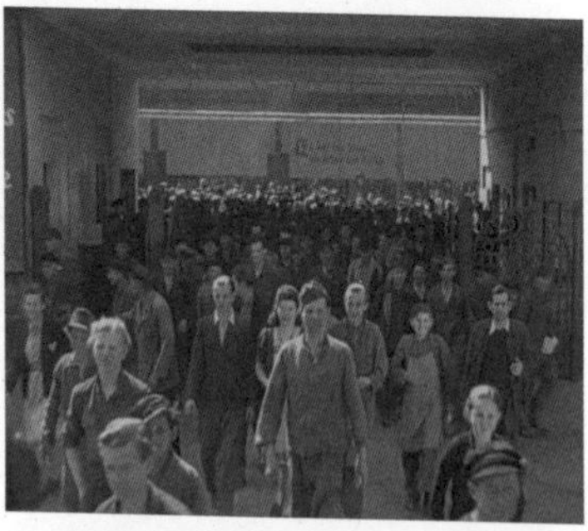

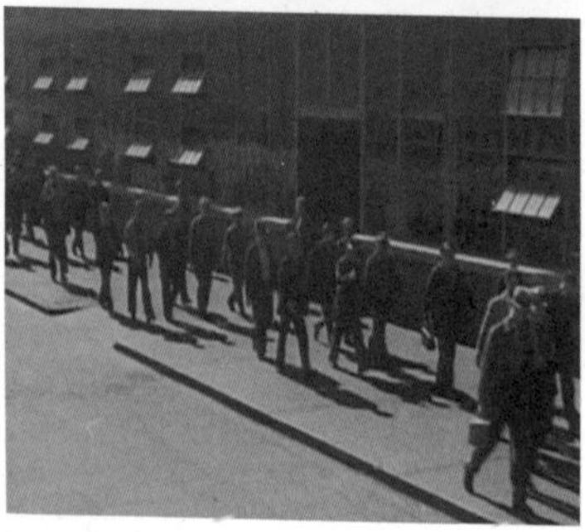

La Sortie de l'usine Lumière à Lyon (Arbeiter verlassen die Lumière-Werke) von Auguste & Louis Lumière, eines der ältesten Dokumente der Filmgeschichte, ist der Ausgangspunkt von Harun Farockis Analyse der Rolle der Arbeit (beziehungsweise der Fabrik als einem Ort der Arbeit) im Film. Die rund einminütige Filmsequenz von 1895 richtet die Kamera auf das Werkstor der Lumière-Werke, einer Fabrik für Filmmaterial, aus dem die Arbeiter*innen – von den Brüdern Lumière für die Aufnahme exakt dirigiert – in die Mittagspause strömen. Diese Szene wurde zu einer immer wiederkehrenden rhetorischen Figur im Film, der Farocki in dieser Collagearbeit durch elf Jahrzehnte der Filmgeschichte nachgeht und dabei auf Fritz Langs Dystopie *Metropolis* ebenso trifft wie auf Charlie Chaplin in *Modern Times* oder Lars von Triers *Dancer in the Dark*.

Am Ein- bzw. Ausgang der Fabrik manifestiert sich die strenge zeitliche Taktung, mit der die industrialisierte Arbeit die Menschen und ihren gesamten Tagesablauf unterwirft. Auch werden hier die einzelnen Arbeiter*innen zu einer organisierten Masse, zur Arbeiterschaft, als dichotomisches Gegenüber der Sphäre des Kapitals. In zahlreichen Industrie- und Propagandafilmen ist es dieser Ort, der Begriffen wie „Proletariat", „Ausbeutung" oder „Massengesellschaft", aber auch den Themen Streik und Arbeitskampf, die Farocki besonders interessieren, ein Bild gibt. Das Werkstor, meist ikonisch mit Gitterstäben dargestellt, zieht sich als Gesellschaft konstituierender Ort durch die Filmgeschichte. Es ist die mit Bedeutungen aufgeladene Grenze zwischen der privaten Sphäre unter Kontrolle des kapitalistischen Unternehmers und dem öffentlichen Raum als Schauplatz des gemeinsamen politischen Ausdrucks. Die Arbeitenden strömen in Eile aus der Arbeit in den Freiraum des Feierabends, fast wie auf der Flucht, während auf der anderen Seite Arbeitsuchende sehnlichst hinein in die Arbeitswelt drängen. Heute ist diese Grenze unscharf geworden, greift eine entgrenzte Arbeitswelt immer stärker in die Freizeit, ins Homeoffice, ins Privatleben ein. (mg)

Harun Farocki

Workers Leaving the Factory, 1995
Video, 4:3; 36 min

Courtesy of Antje Ehmann / Harun Farocki GbR

La Sortie de l'usine Lumière à Lyon (Workers Leaving the Lumière Factory) by Auguste & Louis Lumière, one of the oldest documents in film history, forms the basis for Harun Farocki's analysis of the role of work (or the factory as a place of work) in film. The approximately one-minute film sequence from 1895 points the camera at the gates of the Lumière factory, a manufacturer of film material, as the workers – precisely directed by the Lumière brothers for the shot – stream out for their lunch break. This scene was to become a recurring rhetorical figure in film, traced by Farocki's collage work through eleven decades of film history, touching on Fritz Lang's dystopia *Metropolis* as well as Charlie Chaplin in *Modern Times* and Lars von Trier's *Dancer in the Dark*.

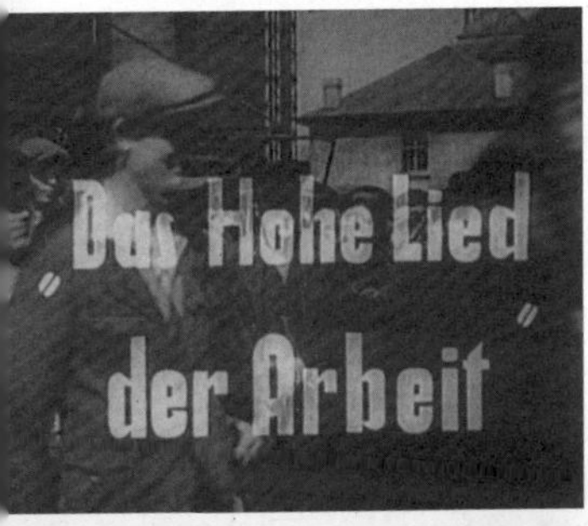

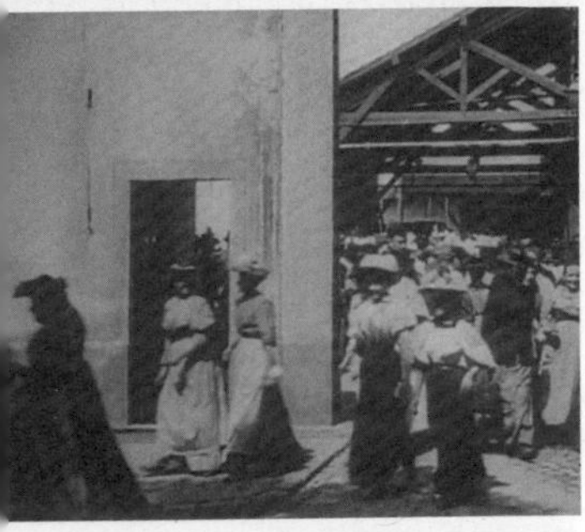

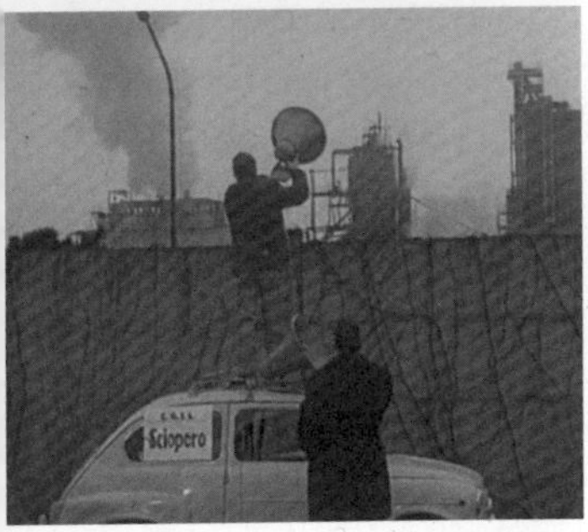

The film of people entering and exiting the factory highlights the strict timetable of industrialised labour dominating their lives and daily routine. Here, the individual workers also become an organised mass, the workforce, as a dichotomous counterpart to the sphere of capital. In many industrial and propaganda films it is this location that provides an image for concepts such as 'the proletariat', 'exploitation' or 'mass society', but also to the themes of strikes and labour dispute, which were of special interest to Farocki. The factory gates, usually depicted with their iconic bars, run through film history as a place that represents society. Charged with meaning, they are the boundary between the private sphere under the control of the capitalist entrepreneur and the public space as the arena of collective political expression. Workers hurry out into the free space of the evening, almost as if they are fleeing, while on the other side jobseekers are desperately trying to push their way into the world of work. Today this boundary has become blurred, with an increasingly borderless working world encroaching on leisure time, the home office and private life. (mg)

Aldo Giannotti

Museum Encounters (On Work), 2024
Dauerperformance

Courtesy des Künstlers

Aldo Giannotti hat eine Vorliebe für das Hinterfragen von Strukturen und stellt die Funktion von Institutionen gerne auf den Prüfstand.
In *Museum as a Gym* etwa erklärte er 2016 das Kunsthaus Graz zum Fitnessstudio, das in Sportkleidung bei freiem Eintritt besucht werden konnte und einen „Fitnessparcours" anbot. Dabei testete er nicht nur die Funktionalität des Museums, sondern auch dessen soziale Belastbarkeit.
Auch die aktuelle Arbeit richtet das Vergrößerungsglas auf die Institution: Während der gesamten Ausstellungsdauer wird ein*e Mitarbeiter*in des Museums täglich für eine Stunde im Ausstellungsraum anwesend sein, um mit den Besucher*innen zu sprechen.
Die Reihe von Begegnungen zwischen Fremden verwandelt den Ausstellungsraum in eine soziale Sphäre, in der die menschliche Interaktion selbst zum Kunstwerk wird. Im Gegensatz zur vorangegangenen Arbeit *Museum Encounter*, die Giannotti 2023 im Rahmen der Ausstellung *Systemrelevant* im Künstlerhaus Wien durchführte und bei der die Gesprächsthemen frei wählbar waren, setzt er hier einen klaren Rahmen für die Diskussion: Es geht um die Kulturarbeit und damit bis zu einem gewissen Grad auch um eine Selbstreflexion der Institution. Welche Berufsfelder braucht es, um eine Ausstellung zu gestalten, Sammlungsstücke zu bewahren und Kunst- und Kulturprojekte umzusetzen und zu vermitteln? Was sind die Highlights unserer täglichen Arbeit, die Kämpfe, Bedingungen, Wünsche, Ängste, Herausforderungen, Vor- und Nachteile?
Obwohl das Thema im Voraus feststeht, wird der Verlauf der Unterhaltung von den Gesprächspartner*innen ausgehandelt; der Künstler stellt lediglich die Infrastruktur zur Verfügung, damit Verbindungen hergestellt werden können. Für jene Besucher*innen, die sich nicht aktiv beteiligen, verwandelt sich die Situation in eine soziale Skulptur. Gleichzeitig unterstreicht das Werk die Bedeutung dessen, was nicht von KI oder Maschinen übernommen werden kann: menschliche Interaktion und Dialog. (kh)

Aldo Giannotti

Museum Encounters (On Work), 2024
Durational performance

Courtesy of the artist

Aldo Giannotti has a penchant for questioning structures and likes to put the function of institutions to the test. In his 2016 work *Museum as a Gym,* for instance, he announced that the Kunsthaus Graz was to become a gym, offering free entry for anyone in sportswear together with a 'fitness course'. This was not just to check the functionality of the museum – its social resilience was also examined.
Giannotti's current work also turns the magnifying glass on the institution: throughout the exhibition, one museum employee will be present in the exhibition space for one hour each day to talk to visitors. This series of encounters between strangers transforms the exhibition space into a social sphere in which human interaction itself becomes a work of art. Unlike his previous work *Museum Encounter,* staged by Giannotti in 2023 as part of the exhibition *Systemrelevant* at Künstlerhaus Wien and offering free choice of discussion themes, here he sets a clear framework for the exchange: it's about cultural work, and so to a certain degree also a self-reflection of the institution. What professional areas are needed to design an exhibition, preserve collection items and realise and communicate art and culture projects? What are the highlights of our daily work, the struggles, conditions, wishes, fears, challenges, the pros and cons?
While this specific theme is defined, the course of the conversation is negotiated by the dialogue partners; the artist merely provides the infrastructure so that connections can be made. For visitors who do not actively participate, the situation becomes a social sculpture. At the same time, the work highlights the significance of what cannot be taken over by AI or machines: human interaction and dialogue. (kh)

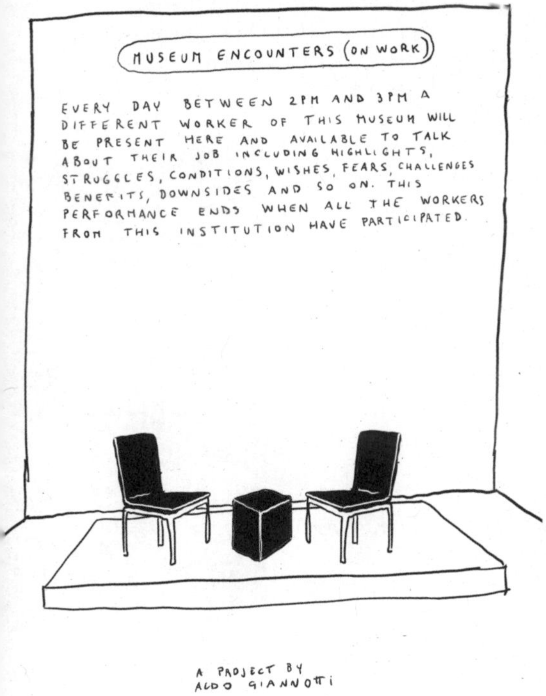

Liam Gillick

The hopes and dreams of the workers as they wandered home from the bar, 2005/2024
Roter Glitter; Maße variabel

Courtesy MEYER*KAINER Wien

Von den Hoffnungen und Träumen der Arbeiter*innen sehen wir auf den ersten Blick nichts. Sie materialisieren sich metaphorisch in deren Fußspuren in einer purpurroten Fläche aus Glitter. Die reduzierte Form, die unmittelbare Präsenz des Materials und die starke, symbolisch aufgeladene Farbe sind typisch für die Arbeit von Liam Gillick. Viele seiner Installationen haben ihren Ursprung in vertrauten, alltäglichen Objekten, die er zu reduzierten architektonischen Settings abstrahiert. Oft haben sie etwas Unvollständiges an sich und erzeugen offene Situationen mit dem Potenzial, etablierte Machtstrukturen zu unterlaufen. Den strengen Minimalismus der Moderne, der sich jeder Narration verweigert, bricht Gillick mit der Andeutung einer Geschichte – oder vielen individuellen Geschichten.
Gillick beschäftigt sich mit Fragen der Ökonomie und Produktion und damit, wie sich deren Bedingungen in der postindustriellen Gesellschaft verändern. Die Organisation von Arbeit und besonders deren soziale Implikationen ziehen sich durch viele seiner künstlerischen Arbeiten wie auch theoretischen Texte.
Der oft mit Geselligkeit und wiederkehrenden Festen assoziierte Glitter ist ein häufiges Motiv in Gillicks Arbeit. Er verweist auf das Gemeinschaftliche, das im Spätkapitalismus sukzessive vom Individualismus abgelöst wurde, und wird zum Symbol für eine zyklische kollektive Erneuerung. 2022 war die Arbeit in der legendären, 1982 geschlossenen Turiner „Lingotto"-Fabrik von FIAT ausgestellt, wo sie die dramatischen Umwälzungen in der Automobilproduktion und die damit einhergehenden Veränderungen der Arbeitssituation der Werktätigen thematisierte. Die Bar wiederum hat eine wesentliche Funktion als dichotomischer Gegenort zur durchgetakteten, an Effizienz und Produktivität orientierten Arbeitswelt. Hier können die Arbeiter*innen bei einem Glas Bier die Zeit vergessen, sie dürfen abschweifen, müssen nicht „funktionieren". Doch auch dieser Rückzugsort von der Arbeitswelt wird von dieser zunehmend durchdrungen, wovon nicht zuletzt die Laptops von Kreativen und Freiberufler*innen in den hippen Cafés und Bars zeugen. Im Kontext des Kunsthauses Graz wird dieser Aspekt der Arbeit Gillicks sichtbar und lässt sie uns noch einmal neu interpretieren. (mg)

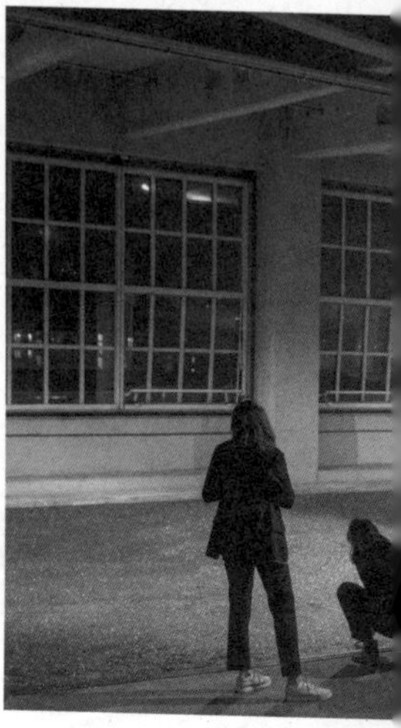

Liam Gillick

The hopes and dreams of the workers as they wandered home from the bar, 2005/2024
Red glitter; variable dimensions

Courtesy of MEYER*KAINER Vienna

On first sight, we can see nothing of the hopes and dreams of the workers. They materialise metaphorically in their footprints in the expanse of crimson glitter. The reduced form, the direct presence of the material and the powerful colour with symbolic charge are typical of Liam Gillick's work. Many of his installations have their origins in familiar, everyday objects which he abstracts into reduced architectural settings. These often have something incomplete about them and generate open situations with the potential to undermine established power structures. He breaks with the strict minimalism in modernism that rejects any narrative by hinting at a story – or many individual stories.
Gillick's work engages with questions of economy and production and how their conditions are changing in post-industrial society. The organisation of work and especially its social implications are a theme that runs through many of his works and theoretical texts. Glitter, a repeated motif in Gillick's work, carries connotations of sociability as well as regular festivities. It refers to the communality that has been gradually superseded by individualism in late capitalism and becomes a symbol of cyclical collective renewal. In 2022 the work was shown at FIAT's legendary 'Lingotto' factory in Turin, which closed down in 1982. Here it explored the dramatic upheavals in automotive production and consequent changes to the labour situation of the workers. Meanwhile the bar mentioned in the title takes on a vital function as dichotomous counter-site to the carefully clocked hours of the working world at the factory or office, which is optimised for efficiency and productivity. Here, workers can forget the time over a few beers, can relax and linger, do not have to 'function'. Yet even this refuge from the world of work is increasingly permeated, as is clearly evidenced by the laptops of creatives and freelancers at hip cafés and bars. In the context of Kunsthaus Graz, this aspect of Gillicks work is visualised, allowing it to be interpreted anew. (mg)

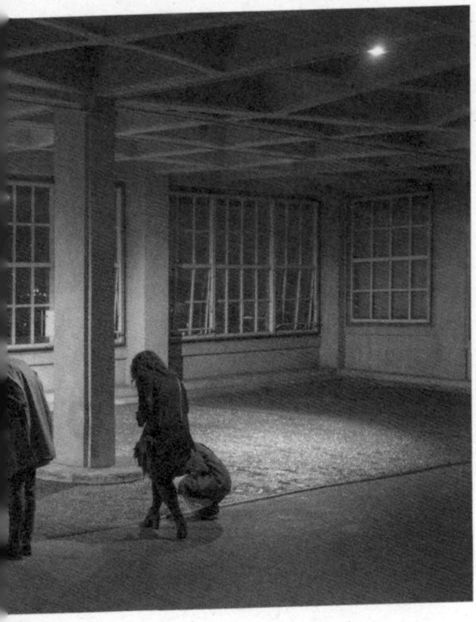

Lisa Großkopf

She Works Hard for the Money, 2023
Holz, Fertigputz, Metall, Kunststoff, Epoxidharz, Springbälle, Münzen; 180 × 250 × 50 cm

Courtesy der Künstlerin

Der etwas aus der Zeit gefallen wirkende Kaugummiautomat an dem grob verputzen Wandfragment lässt unweigerlich nostalgische Erinnerungen an die Kindheitstage aufkommen: Wer kennt nicht den altmodischen Münzeinwurf, den schwergängigen mechanischen Drehknopf und vor allem die Spannung, was man denn für die eingeworfene Zwei-Euro-Münze erhalten würde. Wobei das nur selten Kaugummis sind, sondern meist allerhand mehr oder weniger Brauchbares aus Plastik. Doch nicht der tatsächliche monetäre Wert, sondern genau dieses Spiel mit einer Erwartungshaltung und dem Zufall ist es, was den Reiz solcher Automaten ausmacht – und was auch Lisa Großkopf interessiert.
In ihrer Arbeit eignet sich die Künstlerin Bekanntes, einfache Artefakte aus dem Alltag, oft aus der Welt des Konsums, an und betrachtet sie aus einer gesellschaftskritischen Perspektive. Dem tradierten Idealbild der bunten Überraschung in der Kunststoffkugel stellt sie deren Herstellung gegenüber, die in industrieller Massenproduktion meist unter fragwürdigen und prekären Arbeitsbedingungen in Billiglohnländern erfolgt. Einige der Gegenstände in Großkopfs Automat hingegen sind von ihr selbst in zeitintensiver Handarbeit gefertigte Einzelstücke und mit einer sorgfältig eingepassten 50-Cent-Münze versehen. Mit etwas Glück erhalten wir sofort ein Viertel des Kaufpreises in bar zurück. Ein Verweis auf die omnipräsenten Rabattaktionen, mit denen Konsument*innen gelockt werden. Die Arbeit untersucht die Konstruktion von auseinanderlaufenden Wertvorstellungen und -zuschreibungen: Die von der Künstlerin in die Herstellung investierte Zeit entspricht einem Vielfachen des Verkaufspreises von zwei Euro, während wir uns über die retournierten 50 Cent freuen, die wir so „gespart" haben. In der partizipativen Intervention, die erstmals 2023 im öffentlichen Raum am Lendkanal in Klagenfurt realisiert wurde, überträgt Lisa Großkopf ihre eigene Neugierde auf die vorbeiflanierenden Besucher*innen im Ausstellungsraum. Sie können für zwei Euro Teil einer künstlerischen Wertschöpfungskette zwischen Arbeit, Konsum und Wert werden. (mg)

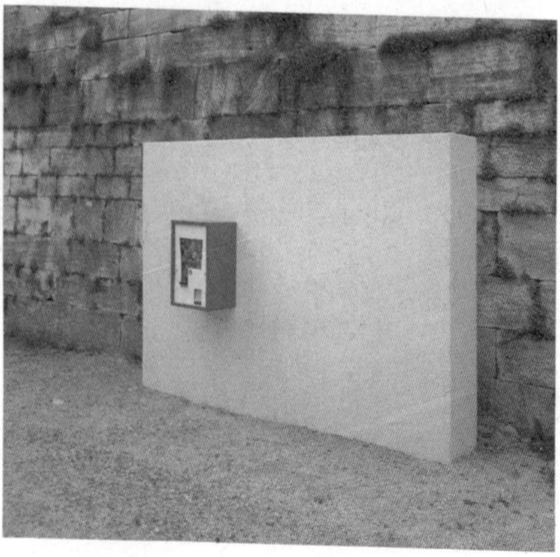

Lisa Großkopf

She Works Hard for the Money, 2023
Wood, finished plaster, metal, plastic, epoxy resin, bouncy balls, coins; 180 × 250 × 50 cm

Courtesy of the artist

Like something from another time, the chewing-gum vending machine on the roughly plastered section of wall carries nostalgic memories of childhood days: who doesn't remember the old-fashioned coin slot, the stiff mechanical knob and, above all, the excitement of wondering what you would get for your two-euro coin. Although it is rarely chewing gum, but usually all sorts of plastic trinkets of variable usefulness. However, it is not the actual monetary value but rather this play on expectations and luck that makes these vending machines so appealing – and which also interests Lisa Großkopf.
The artist appropriates familiar simple artefacts from everyday life, often from the world of consumption, and examines them from a socio-critical perspective. She contrasts the traditional ideal image of the colourful surprise in the plastic ball with its mass production under questionable and precarious working conditions in low-wage countries. Some of the objects in Großkopf's vending machine are instead unique pieces that she painstakingly handcrafts herself and include a carefully fitted 50-cent coin. With a bit of luck, we might get a quarter of the price we paid straight back in cash. A reference to the ubiquitous discount campaigns employed to lure consumers. The work explores the construction of divergent value concepts and attributions: the time invested by the artist in production corresponds to a multiple of the price of two euros, while we are happy about the returned 50 cents that we have 'saved' in this way. In the participatory intervention, which was realised for the first time in 2023 in public space at the Lendkanal in Klagenfurt, Lisa Großkopf transfers her own curiosity to visitors walking past in the exhibition space. For two euros, they can become part of an artistic value chain between work, consumption and value. (mg)

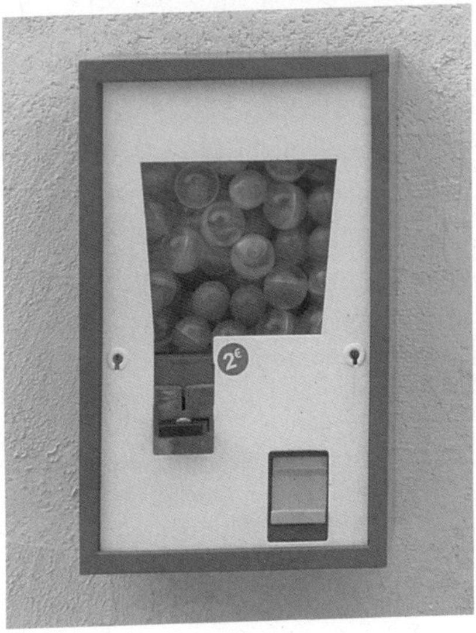

Andreas Gursky

Amazon, 2016
C-Print Diasec; gerahmt 207 × 407 × 6 cm

Courtesy Privatsammlung Wien / Sprüth Magers

Konsum, Globalisierung und die vielfältigen Phänomene der Massengesellschaft sind ein wesentlicher Untersuchungsgegenstand im Werk des Fotografen Andreas Gursky. *Amazon* zeigt eine schier unendliche Masse an Paketen, Päckchen und bunten Artikeln aller Art in einem Amazon-Verteilzentrum in Phoenix, Arizona. Die (scheinbare) Individualität, die die Konsumgesellschaft uns allen verspricht, eine Welt des Überflusses und der Verschwendung, findet sich in vielen Arbeiten Gurskys, wie etwa auch in den unendlich erscheinenden Supermarktregalen in *99 Cent* (1999), das in *Amazon* ein perfektes Gegenüber findet. Gursky bleibt in seiner Arbeit stets der genaue und kritische Beobachter, der aber nie direkt kritisiert oder wertet. Die prekären Arbeitsbedingungen der unzähligen schlecht bezahlten Angestellten, die täglich Hunderte Pakete für den Versand zusammenstellen, sind im menschenleer abgebildeten Lager nicht sichtbar. Sie erschließen sich erst vor unserem geistigen Auge, dazu angeregt auch durch die abgebildeten Leitgedanken des Unternehmens, die auch zynisch gelesen werden können: „work hard", „have fun", „make history" und – nicht auf dem Foto – „deliver results".

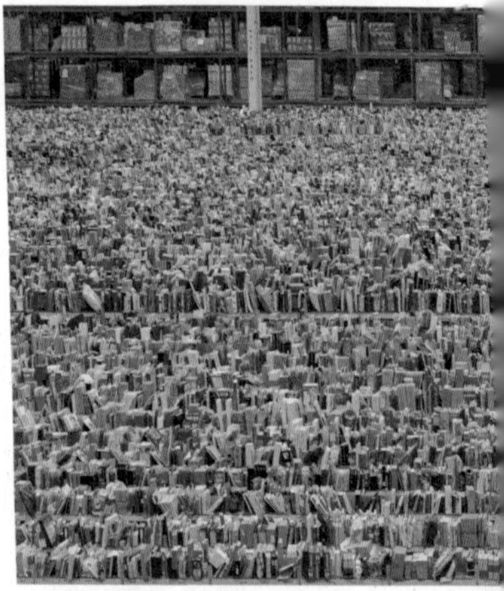

In seinen streng komponierten Bildern, die immer eine Distanz zum Gegenstand behalten, ist die dokumentarische Praxis von Bernd und Hilla Becher, den Ikonen der Architekturfotografie, deren Studierender Gursky war, unverkennbar. Er erweitert deren präzise Großformattechik jedoch um die digitale Bildbearbeitung und die Bildmontage. Gursky kombiniert viele Hunderte Aufnahmen desselben Ortes zu einem einzigen Bild von enormem Detailreichtum. Aus der Distanz ein faszinierendes formalistisches Ornament der Masse, offenbart die Fotografie aus der Nähe eine Vielzahl an individuellen Aspekten und Geschichten. Die meist strenge Konstruktion und extreme Verflachung des Bildes, die er unter anderem über unterschiedliche Brennweiten der Einzelbilder erreicht, machen die Manipulation offen sichtbar.

Gurskys Spiel mit „Monumentalität und Intimität" (Hanno Rauterberg) verleiht dem Spezifischen eine Allgemeingültigkeit, die keinen herkömmlichen Authentizitätsanspruch stellt. Seine Bildmanipulationen verändern den Inhalt der Fotografien nicht, sondern verdichten die Wirklichkeit, überhöhen, an Alte Meister erinnernd, die Realität. (mg)

Andreas Gursky

Amazon, 2016
C-Print Diasec; framed 207 × 407 × 6 cm

Courtesy of Private Collection Vienna / Sprüth Magers

Consumption, globalisation and the diverse phenomena of mass society are a key subject investigated in the work of photographer Andreas Gursky. *Amazon* shows a near endless mass of parcels, packages and multi-coloured array of articles in an Amazon distribution centre in Phoenix, Arizona. The (apparent) individuality held out as a promise to us all by consumer society, a world of abundance and waste, is to be found in many of Gursky's works, such as in the almost endless supermarket shelves in *99 Cent* (1999), which finds a perfect counterpart in *Amazon*.
Gursky always maintains the position of a careful and critical observer while never offering direct criticism or judgement in his work. The precarious working conditions of the countless badly paid employees who prepare hundreds of parcels for shipping every day are not visible here in the deserted warehouse. And yet they are clear in the mind's eye, also inspired by the company's guiding principles, which can be read cynically: 'work hard', 'have fun', 'make history' and – not in the photo – 'deliver results'.

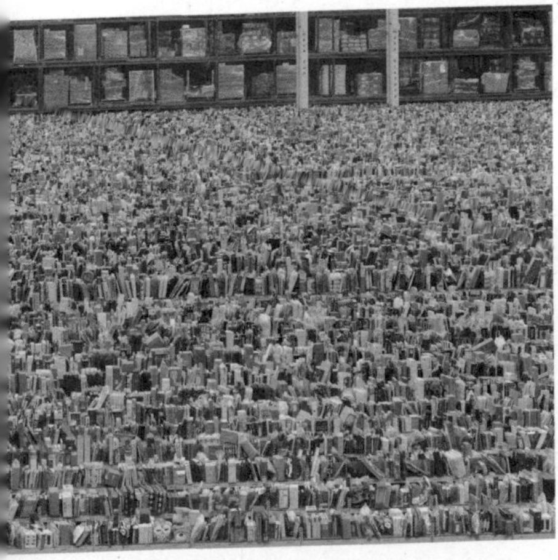

Gursky was a student of Bernd and Hilla Becher, the icons of architectural photography, and their documentary practice is unmistakable in his strictly composed images, which always maintain a distance from the subject. He expands their precise large-format technique to encompass digital image processing and image montage. Gursky combines many hundreds of photographs of the same place into a single image with a huge wealth of detail. From a distance, a fascinating formalistic ornament of the masses, the photograph reveals a multitude of individual aspects and narratives up close. The manipulation is made visible by the largely rigorous structure and extreme flattening of the image, which is achieved in part by using different focal lengths for the individual images.
Gursky's play on 'monumentality and intimacy' (Hanno Rauterberg) gives the specific a universality that does not make a conventional claim to authenticity. His manipulations of the image do not alter the content of the photographs, but instead condense reality, exaggerating it in a way that is reminiscent of the Old Masters. (mg)

Theresa Hattinger, Michael Hieslmair, Michael Zinganel

Pro Line (Hi Vis – No Vis). Hommage an Otto Neurath und Gerd Arntz, 2024
Arbeitsbekleidung, Warnschutzwesten, Bundhosen, Aluminiumrohre, Gehörschutz, MP3-Player, Audiodatei; Sprecher: Herbert Gnauer

Windhosen: Richtungswechsel, 2024
Arbeitsbekleidung, Latzhosen, Aluminiumrohre, Fahnenmasten

Courtesy der Künstler*innen
Unterstützt von CWS Hygiene Österreich GmbH

Die Gebrauchsspuren auf der schon benutzten Arbeitsbekleidung in den Installationen von Theresa Hattinger, Michael Hieslmair und Michael Zinganel im Ausstellungsraum und an den Fahnenmasten vor dem Kunsthaus zeugen von harter, physischer und schmutzig machender Arbeit. Arbeit, die tagtäglich 24/7 geleistet werden muss, um unser angenehmes Leben zu ermöglichen: die Zustellung von immer mehr Waren in die eigenen vier Wände, die Entsorgung der stetig anwachsenden Abfallmengen, „just-in-time"-Anlieferungen in große Produktionsbetriebe. Diese städtischen Infrastrukturen zur Ver- und Entsorgung – riesige Warenumschlagplätze, Lager- und Verteilerzentren – werden immer weiter an die Stadtränder und über sie hinaus an Verkehrsknotenpunkten verlagert, aus der Wahrnehmung ihrer Nutznießer*innen ausgeblendet und verdrängt.
Trotz einer „Logistik 4.0" sind es weiterhin Menschen aus unterschiedlichsten sozialen Milieus, von bestens ausgebildeten Expats bis zu prekär beschäftigen Migrant*innen, die den Warenaustausch organisieren, Lagerhaltung optimieren, Fahrzeuge steuern, Waren ein- und ausladen. Für sie stellen die vermeintlichen Nicht-Orte an der Peripherie mit Geschichte(n) sinnstiftend aufgeladene Lebenswelten dar. Ihre Geschichten sind es, die die Künstler*innen der interdisziplinären Forschungsplattform Tracing Spaces interessieren. Sie untersuchen Orte wie den Logistik-Cluster Kalsdorf, das Cargo Center Graz und den Wiener Nordwestbahnhof und machen einzelne Schicksale, langjährige Firmengeschichten, bemerkenswerte Mikroökonomien der legalen und „grauen" Gewerbe über Gespräche mit den Protagonist*innen erfahrbar. Die Installationen aus typischer, aus Sicherheitsgründen gut sichtbarer Arbeitsbekleidung der Marke *Pro Line HighVis* konterkarieren die Unsichtbarkeit, die die Arbeitenden erfahren. In Anspielung auf den Ökonomen Otto Neurath, der in den 1920er-Jahren mit dem Grafiker Gerd Arntz die „Wiener Methode der Bildstatistik" zur Veranschaulichung komplexer Sachverhalte durch farbige Männchen entwickelte, schufen Hattinger, Hieslmair und Zinganel für die Ausstellung eine Visualiserung der Migrations- und Mobilitätserfahrungen aus dem Milieu der endlosen Logistiklandschaften, ohne die unsere Städte nicht existieren könnten. (mg)

Theresa Hattinger, Michael Hieslmair, Michael Zinganel

Pro Line (Hi Vis – No Vis). Hommage an Otto Neurath und Gerd Arntz, 2024
Work clothing, high-visibility waistcoats, trousers, aluminium tubes, hearing protection, MP3 player, audio file; narrator: Herbert Gnauer

Windhosen: Richtungswechsel, 2024
Work clothing, dungarees, aluminium pipes, flagpoles

Courtesy of the artists
Supported by CWS Hygiene Österreich GmbH

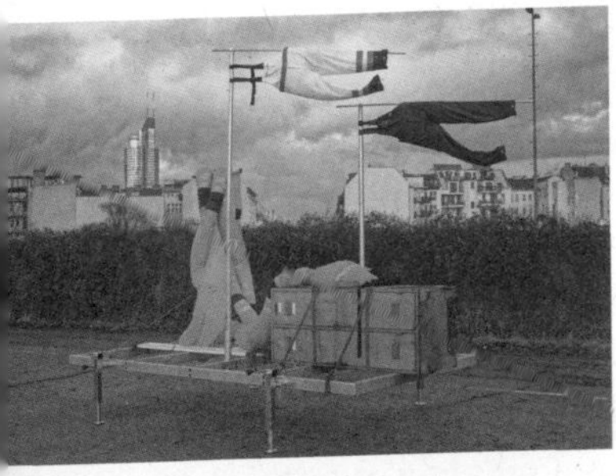

The traces of use on the work clothes in the installations by Theresa Hattinger, Michael Hieslmair and Michael Zinganel in the exhibition space and on the flagpoles in front of the Kunsthaus are proof of hard and dirty work. Work that has to be done every single day 24/7 to make our comfortable lives possible: the shipping of ever more goods straight to our homes, the disposal of constantly rising amounts of waste, 'just-in-time' deliveries to large manufacturing plants. These infrastructures for goods supply and waste disposal – vast transhipment centres, warehouses and distribution points – have been shifted further and further beyond the city limits to transport hubs in the outskirts, erased from the awareness of their recipients. Despite the ever-evolving 'Logistics 4.0', it is still people from diverse social milieus, from highly educated expats through to precariously employed migrants, who organise the exchange of goods, optimise warehousing, drive vehicles and load and unload goods. For these people, the apparent non-places on the periphery constitute a living environment charged with meaning and (hi)stories.
It is their stories that interest the artists of the interdisciplinary research platform Tracing Spaces. They examine places such as the Kalsdorf logistics cluster, the Cargo Center Graz and Vienna's Nordwestbahnhof railway station and make the individual fates, long company histories and remarkable micro-economies of the legal and 'grey' areas of commerce tangible through conversations with the protagonists. The installations made of typical *Pro Line HighVis* workwear, which is highly visible for safety reasons, counteract the invisibility that workers experience. Alluding to the economist Otto Neurath, who in the 1920s developed the 'Viennese method of pictorial statistics' with the graphic artist Gerd Arntz to illustrate complex facts using coloured figures, Hattinger, Hieslmair and Zinganel created a visualisation of migration and mobility experiences from the milieu of endless logistics landscapes, without which our cities could not exist. (mg)

Tehching Hsieh

One Year Performance, 1980–1981
Dokumentation der Dauerperformance; Auszüge, Erklärungen, fehlende Stempelkarte, Fotos, Zeitkarte, digitalisierter 16-mm-Film, Poster; Maße variabel

Courtesy des Künstlers

Der taiwanesisch-amerikanische Performancekünstler Tehching Hsieh kam 1974 ohne Papiere nach New York und lebte dort bis zu seiner Einbürgerung im Jahr 1988 täglich mit der Angst, in sein Heimatland Taiwan abgeschoben zu werden. Ab 1978 führte er eine Serie von fünf einjährigen Selbstversuchen zum Thema Ausdauer durch, in denen er die Grenzen des Menschen testete. Die Performance *Time Clock Piece* war seine zweite *One Year Performance*.
Vom 11. April 1980 bis zum 11. April 1981 betätigte Tehching Hsieh zu jeder vollen Stunde eine in seinem New Yorker Atelier installierte Stempeluhr und nahm dabei gleichzeitig ein Bild von sich auf 16-mm-Film auf. Hsieh hatte sich vorgenommen, 365 Tage lang 24 Mal am Tag zu stempeln. Der damit einhergehende unvermeidliche Schlafentzug versetzte den Künstler in einen Zustand des Wachdeliriums, was unter anderem dazu führte, dass einige Aufnahmen misslangen. Rückblickend sagte Hsieh, er habe sich in jenem Jahr wie Sisyphos gefühlt – beschäftigt mit einer sinnlosen Aufgabe, die seinem Leben dennoch Sinn und Struktur gab. Die Uniform, die Tehching Hsieh während des *Time Clock Piece* trägt, verstärkt die Assoziation mit der Arbeitswelt, an der er offiziell nicht teilnehmen durfte. Gleichzeitig betont sie die Idee der Selbstregulierung und Disziplin und verweist auf die Unsichtbarkeit, die häufig mit der Migration in ein unbekanntes Umfeld einhergeht.
Die Verpflichtung, sich selbst zu stempeln, widerspiegelt die ständige Überwachung und Unsicherheit, die mit Hsiehs prekärer Situation einherging. Darüber hinaus verweist der sich wiederholende Akt des Stempelns auf die Zwänge und Routinen des Arbeitslebens und stellt gleichzeitig die fragilen Grenzen zwischen Arbeit, Leben und Kunst infrage.
Als physische Manifestation dieser intensiven Selbstbeobachtung und Konzentration auf die Zeit erstellte Hsieh 8.666 Zeitkarten (für die verbleibenden 94 hatte er den Zeitpunkt verschlafen). „Zeit zu verschwenden ist mein Konzept des Lebens", erklärte der Künstler Jahrzehnte später in einem Interview. „Leben ist nichts anderes als Zeit zu verbrauchen, bis man stirbt." (kh)

Tehching Hsieh

One Year Performance, 1980–1981
Documentation of the durational performance; statements, explanations, missing punch record, photographs, timecard, digitised 16 mm film, poster; variable dimnensions

Courtesy of the artist

The Taiwanese-American performance artist Tehching Hsieh arrived in New York as an illegal immigrant in 1974, and had to live every day with the fear of being deported back to his home country of Taiwan until he was naturalised in 1988. He processed his feelings of isolation and the fear of prison and deportation in his first *One Year Performance in* 1978/79, the beginning of a three-year self-experiment in perseverance.
From 11 April 1980 to 11 April 1981, Tehching Hsieh punched a time clock installed in his New York studio every hour on the hour while simultaneously taking a picture of himself on 16 mm film. Hsieh had set himself the goal of clocking in 24 times a day for 365 days. The inevitable sleep deprivation this required put the artist in a state of waking delirium, which, among other things, led to some shots failing. Looking back, Hsieh said he felt like Sisyphus that year – occupied with a pointless task that did nonetheless give his life some meaning and structure. The uniform that Tehching Hsieh wears during the *Time Clock Piece* amplifies the association with the world of work in which he could not officially participate. At the same time, it underlines the idea of self-regulation and discipline and refers to the anonymity that often accompanies immigrants in a foreign environment.
The obligation to clock in reflects the constant surveillance and insecurity that accompanied Hsieh's precarious situation. Further to this, the repetitive act of punching in refers to the constraints and routines of working life, while at the same time questioning the fragile boundaries between work, life and art.
As a physical manifestation of this intense self-observation and concentration on time, Hsieh created 8,666 time cards (he had slept through the time for the remaining 94). 'Wasting time is my concept of life', the artist explained in an interview decades later. 'Living is nothing but consuming time until you die.' (kh)

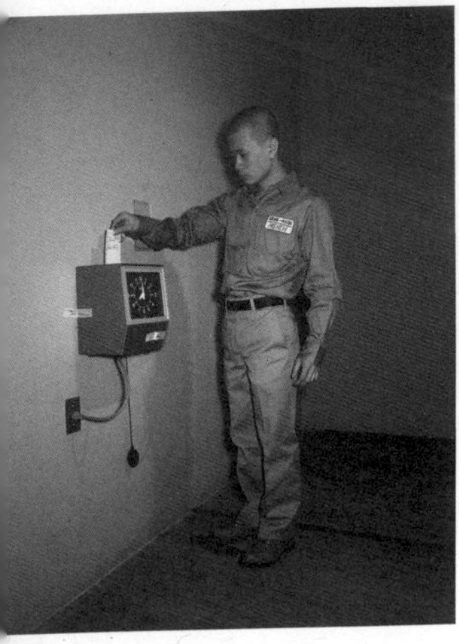

Johanna Kandl

Prospektor, 2021
Tempera auf Holz; 170 × 250 cm

Carry On, 2023
Tempera auf Holz; 100 × 70 cm

Courtesy Helmut & Johanna Kandl

Das Medium von Johanna Kandl ist die Malerei – und alles andere. Ob sie sich auf dem Bildträger oder im Video manifestieren, ihre Arbeiten, die meist in Zusammenarbeit mit ihrem Mann Helmut Kandl entstehen, sind geprägt von einer Mischung aus unterschiedlichen Perspektiven, künstlerischer Recherche, persönlichen Geschichten und wissenschaftlichen Aussagen. Seit einigen Jahren ist die Beschäftigung der Künstlerin mit Malmaterialien und deren Herkunft eine bestimmende Konstante in ihrem Werk. Unter Einbeziehung ökonomischer, ökologischer und sozialer Fragestellungen, die sich beispielsweise mit den Arbeitsbedingungen von Minenarbeiter*innen weltweit beschäftigen, entstehen Videos, Bücher, Fotografien, Malerei und ganze Ausstellungen (wie *Palette* im Kunsthaus Graz, 2021/22). Für die Entwicklung ihres vielfältigen Œuvres reist das Künstler*innenpaar an entlegene Orte, an denen Pigmente und andere Werkstoffe abgebaut, Pinsel oder Leinen erzeugt werden.
Prospektor zeigt einen Bergmann inmitten einer kargen Landschaft in Marokko in der Nähe der großen alten Kobaltmine in Bou Azzer bei Ouarzazate. Kawtar Tansui, eine junge Geologin der Mine, und ihr Kollege fuhren mit Johanna Kandl auf den Berg, um ihr einen Blick auf die Abbaustelle zu ermöglichen. Die Hitze, die förmlich aus dem großformatigen Bild strömt, wird durch den lapidaren Satz am unteren Bildrand („... zur selben Zeit in einem klimatisierten Büro") unterstrichen. Die so angedeutete Ungleichheit erzählt von den unterschiedlichen Lebensrealitäten jener, die den harten und gefährlichen Arbeitsbedingungen im Bergbau ausgesetzt sind, und dem internationalem Rohstoffhandel.
Das erst kürzlich entstandene Gemälde *Carry On* zeigt eine Frau in der aserbaidschanischen Provinz vor einem Mosaik aus der Sowjetzeit. Auch hier gibt es eine Parallelhandlung. Die Realität sieht anders aus als die auf dem Mosaik im Hintergrund idealisierte Sowjetwelt. Der hinzugefügte Satz schafft eine weitere Bedeutungsebene: „Carry on" bezieht sich auf das Tragen der Last und das unermüdliche eigene künstlerische Wirken. „Carry on" kann aber auch als Aufforderung verstanden werden, trotz aller politischen, wirtschaftlichen und sozialen Schwierigkeiten „weiterzumachen". (kh)

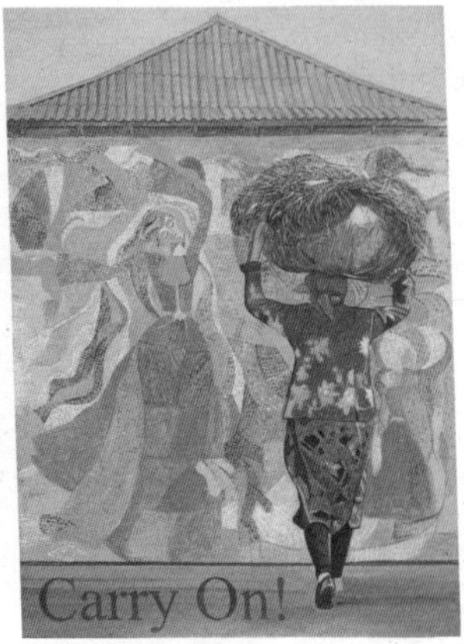

Carry On, 2023

Johanna Kandl

Prospector, 2021
Tempera on wood; 170 × 250 cm

Carry On, 2023
Tempera on wood; 100 × 70 cm

Courtesy Helmut & Johanna Kandl

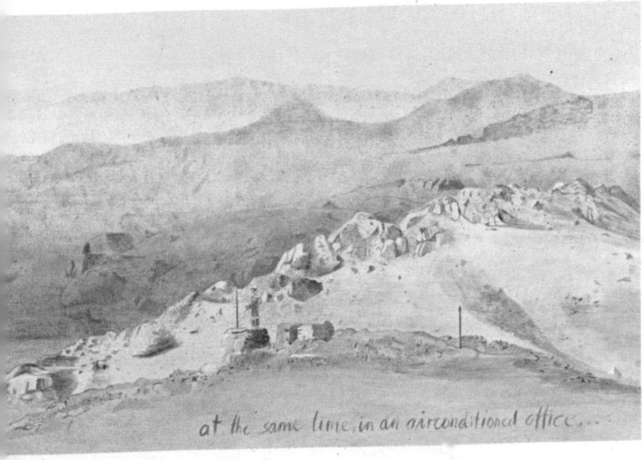

Prospector, 2021

Johanna Kandl's medium is painting – and everything else. Whether they are executed on the picture base or as video, her works, usually created in collaboration with her husband Helmut Kandl, display a blend of different perspectives, artistic research, personal stories and scientific statements. For several years now, the artist's fascination with painting materials and their origins has been a defining constant in her work. Exploring economic, ecological and social issues, such as the working conditions of miners across the world, she creates videos, books, photographs, paintings and entire exhibitions (such as *Palette* at Kunsthaus Graz, 2021/22). The artist duo develop their diverse oeuvre by travelling to remote places where pigments and other materials are mined and brushes or linen are made.

Prospector shows a miner standing in the middle of an arid landscape in Morocco near the large old cobalt mine at Bou Azzer near Ouarzazate. Kawtar Tansui, a young geologist at the mine, and her colleague drove to the top of the mountain with Johanna Kandl to show her a view of the mining site. The heat that virtually pours out of the large-format image is emphasised by the succinct phrase at the bottom of the picture ('... at the same time in an air-conditioned office'). This implied inequality tells of the different realities of life: on the one hand those who are exposed to the harsh and dangerous working conditions in mining – and on the other hand the international trade in raw materials.

Her recent painting *Carry On* shows a woman in Azerbaijan in front of a Soviet-era mosaic. Here, too, we see a parallel plot. Reality looks very different from the idealised Soviet world of the mosaic in the background. The phrase added at the bottom generates another layer of meaning: 'Carry on' refers to the carrying of the load and also Kandl's own tireless artistic endeavours. It can however also be understood as a call to 'carry on' in spite of all the political, economic and social difficulties. (kh)

Peter Kogler

Ohne Titel, 1992/2024
Siebdruck auf Papier; Maße variabel

Courtesy des Künstlers

Peter Kogler ist bekannt für seine digitale Kunst. Seine Werke zeichnen sich durch wiederholte Motive aus, die in alle Richtungen erweitert werden können. Er verwendet Computer, um Ameisen, Röhren, Gehirne oder Weltkugeln zu generieren, die er dann oft im Siebdruckverfahren ausführt. Diese Motive sind in vielen öffentlichen und oft betriebsamen Räumen zu finden und bilden ein Spiel zwischen verwirrenden Labyrinthen und dekorativen Ornamenten. Seine Entscheidung, einem seriellen Prinzip zu folgen, widerspiegelt die Realität, dass viele Dinge in unserer Gesellschaft in großen Stückzahlen hergestellt werden. Dabei treten Kogler selbst und seine persönliche Handschrift zurück und er betont, dass Kunst reproduzierbar und sogar standardisierbar ist.
Kogler entdeckte das Motiv der Ameise vor mehr als 40 Jahren, als er eines der Insekten beobachtete, das über eine Zeitung kroch und dabei wie ein Buchstabe aussah, der sich verselbstständigt hatte. Jahre später, 1992, tapezierte er die Gänge des Fridericianums auf der Documenta 9 in Kassel mit kreuz und quer verlaufenden Ameisenstraßen. Der zeichenhafte Charakter der Ameise und die damit verbundene Information sind seither ein wiederkehrendes Thema. Zum Auftakt der Ausstellung dienen Koglers Ameisen als Metapher für harte Arbeit, Kooperation und Organisation. Mit unermüdlichem Fleiß und in kollektiven Gemeinschaften arbeiten Ameisen zusammen, wobei jedes Insekt eine bestimmte Funktion übernimmt, was es ihnen ermöglicht, komplexe Aufgaben effizient zu erledigen. (kh)

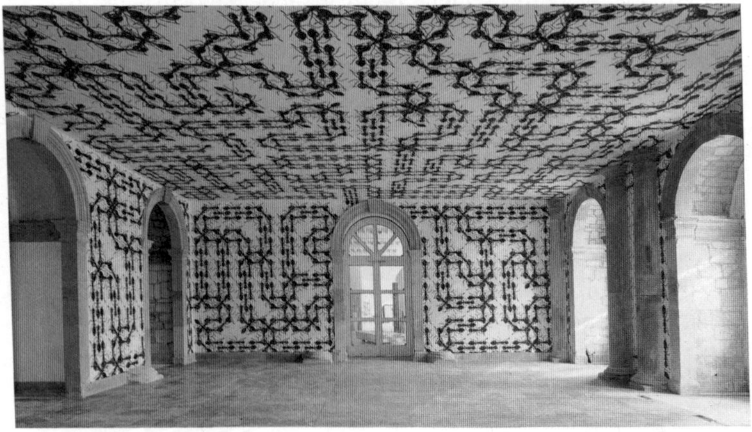

Ausstellungsansicht Installation view, Documenta IX, Kassel, 1992

Peter Kogler

Untitled, 1992/2024
Silkscreen on paper; variable dimensions

Courtesy of the artist

Peter Kogler is famous for his digital art. His works are characterised by repeated motifs that can be extended in all directions. He uses a computer to generate ants, tubes, brains and globes, which he then often screen-prints. These motifs can be found in many public and generally busy spaces, and create a play between confusing labyrinths and decorative ornaments. His decision to follow a serial principle echoes the reality that many things in our society are manufactured in large numbers. Kogler himself and his personal signature take a back seat, signalling that art can be reproduced and even standardised.
Kogler discovered the ant motif over forty years ago when he watched one of these insects crawling over newspaper, as if a printed letter had taken on a life of its own. Years later, in 1992, he installed a wallpaper of criss-crossing ant trails through the corridors of the Fridericianum at Documenta 9 in Kassel. Ever since, the symbolic nature of the ant and associated facts have recurred as a theme in his work. At the start of the exhibition, Kogler's ants serve as a metaphor for hard work, cooperation and organisation. Working with untiring diligence in collective communities the ants collaborate, each insect taking on a specific function that allows them to complete complex tasks efficiently. (kh)

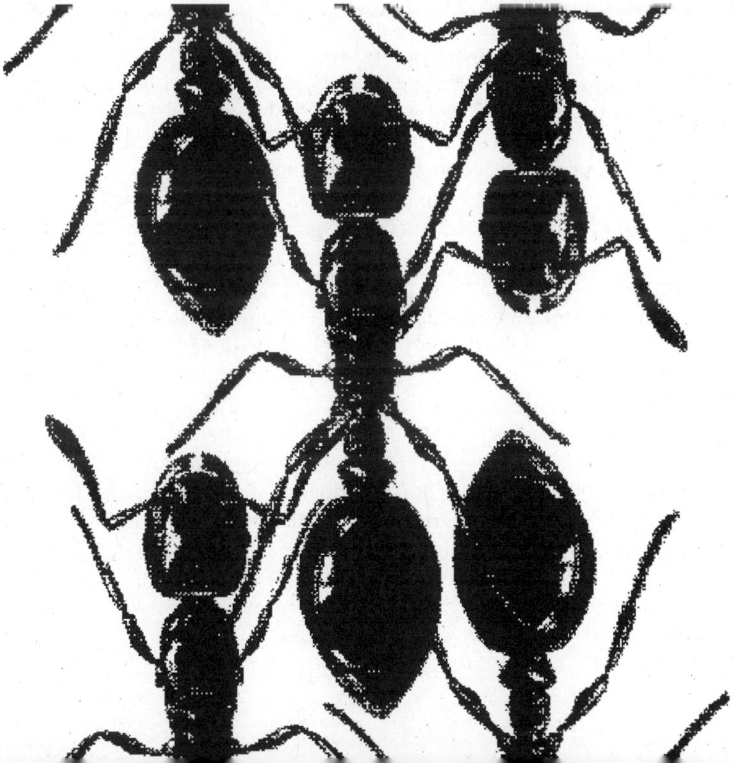

KURS (Mirjana Radovanović, Miloš Miletić)

We have always received something in exchange that we lived.*
On laziness, 2024
**On bourgeois belief*, Bertolt Brecht
Wandbild, Mixed Media; Maße variabel

Courtesy der Künstler*innen

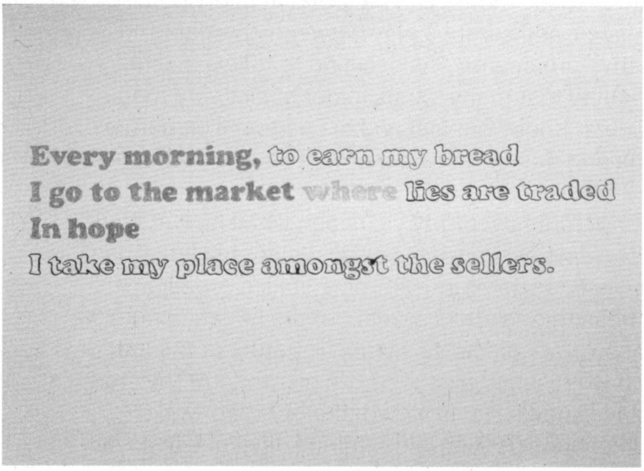

Unter dem Namen KURS erforschen Mirjana Radovanović und Miloš Miletić gemeinsam künstlerische und forschungsbasierte Projekte, die das Potenzial künstlerischer Praxis zur Teilnahme an sozialen Bewegungen untersuchen. Ihre Arbeiten umfassen Wandbilder, Illustrationen und verschiedene Druckerzeugnisse wie Zeitungen, Plakate oder Grafiken und sind zugänglich und verständlich gestaltet.
Die Wandinstallation von KURS für die Ausstellung *24/7* ist ein dreiphasiger Prozess. Die Annäherung an das Thema Arbeit erfolgt über ein Motiv, das im Laufe der Geschichte der westlichen Zivilisation in einen negativen Kontext als eine Form destruktiven Verhaltens gebracht wurde: die Faulheit. In der heutigen Gesellschaft des Spätkapitalismus und der Aufmerksamkeitsökonomie gibt es nur wenige Tätigkeiten, die nicht produktiv sind und sich nicht in irgendeiner Form finanziell verwerten lassen. Doch was würde passieren, wenn wir untätig wären? Ist das heute überhaupt noch möglich? Für wen und warum arbeiten wir so viel und produzieren ständig neue Waren und Inhalte? Ist Faulheit ein Problem oder ist sie eine Art und Weise, wie unser Körper und unser Geist versuchen, sich gegen aufgezwungene Produktivität und Burnout zu wehren? KURS sucht nach Antworten auf diese Fragen und befreit Arbeit, Freizeit und Faulheit von auferlegten Bedeutungen in verschiedenen Epochen und geografischen Räumen.
Die schrittweise Entstehung des Wandbildes während der Ausstellung ist ein Lernprozess, bei dem das Künstler*innenduo in drei Phasen die visuelle Komposition aufbaut, ausgehend von Schlüsseltexten und ergänzt durch ihre Reflexionen über den Begriff der Arbeit. (kh)

KURS (Mirjana Radovanović, Miloš Miletić)

We have always received something in exchange that we lived.*
On laziness, 2024
**On bourgeois belief*, Bertolt Brecht
Mural, mixed media; variable dimensions

Courtesy of the artists

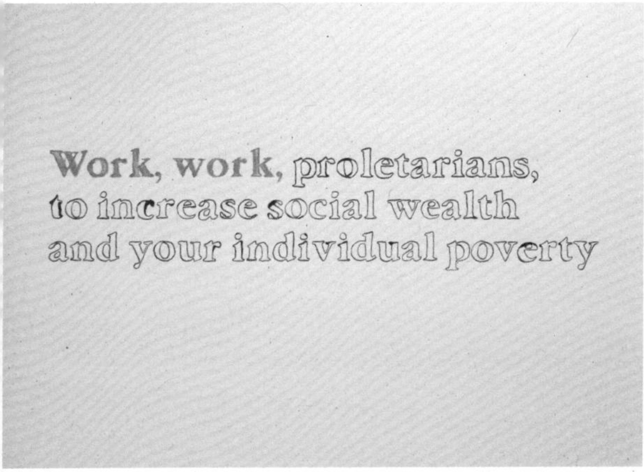

Under the name KURS, Mirjana Radovanović and Miloš Miletić work on joint artistic and research-based projects that examine the potential for artistic practice to be involved in social movements. Their work includes murals, illustrations and a range of printed materials such as newspapers, posters and graphics and is designed to be accessible and understandable. KURS's wall installation for the exhibition *24/7* is a three-phase process. Their investigation of the theme of work is based on a motif which, over the course of the history of Western civilisation, has been placed in a negative context as a form of destructive behaviour: laziness. In today's society of late capitalism and the attention economy, there are few activities that are not productive and which cannot be monetised in some way. But what would happen if we did nothing? Is that even possible nowadays? For whom and why do we work so much, constantly producing new goods and content? Is laziness a problem, or is it how our bodies and minds try to defend themselves against forced productivity and burnout? KURS looks for answers to these questions and liberates work, leisure and laziness from imposed meanings in different eras and geographical spaces. The gradual creation of the mural during the exhibition is a learning process in which the artist duo develops the visual composition in three phases, based on key texts while adding their reflections on the concept of work. (kh)

Shouldn't you

WORK **IN** PROGRESS
ARBEIT

Silvio Lorusso

Shouldn't you be working?, 2016/2024
Aufkleber, Banner; 3,5 × 21 cm, 600 × 750 cm

Courtesy des Künstlers

Wer kennt das nicht: Man ist müde von der Arbeit, macht eine kurze Pause und landet auf Facebook, Instagram oder TikTok, bevor man erst nach viel zu langer Zeit zurückkommt und sich fragt, was man eigentlich den ganzen Nachmittag gemacht hat. StayFocusd, ein Browser-Plugin mit mehr als einer halben Million Nutzer*innen, ist die digitale Lösung, wenn die Zeitverschwendung auf sozialen Medien und anderen Websites außer Kontrolle gerät. Ein großer weißer Bildschirm ersetzt die Oberfläche der betreffenden Zeitverschwendungs-Websites, auf dem der Text „Shouldn't you be working?" (Solltest du nicht arbeiten?) erscheint.
Aber warum sollten wir nur vor dem Bildschirm daran erinnert werden, dass wir nur zu gerne prokrastinieren?
Silvio Lorussos Serie *Shouldn't you be working?* besteht aus Aufklebern, die in einer schnörkellosen, operativen Schrift auf weißem Hintergrund gedruckt sind und in jeder freien oder halbfreien Umgebung – vom Laptop über den Kühlschrank bis zur Toilette – angebracht werden können, um als ständige Erinnerung an die anstehenden Arbeitspflichten zu dienen. Natürlich ist hier die Grenze zwischen Sarkasmus und praktischem Ratschlag fließend: Sie können darüber lachen oder sich wieder in den produktiven Modus versetzen lassen. (kh)

be working?

Silvio Lorusso

Shouldn't you be working?, 2016/2024
Sticker, banner; 3.5 × 21 cm, 600 × 750 cm

Courtesy of the artist

We all know the feeling: you're tired from work, take a short break and end up on Facebook, Instagram or TikTok, but spend far too long there and ask yourself what you've actually been doing all afternoon. To prevent time-wasting on social media and other websites, the digital solution is StayFocusd – a browser plugin with over half a million users. A large white screen replaces the interface of the websites in question, displaying the text: 'Shouldn't you be working?'
But why should it only be on screen that we receive a message to remind us we are only too happy to procrastinate?
Silvio Lorusso's series *Shouldn't you be working?* consists of stickers printed in a plain functional font on a white background. These can be placed in any free or half-free environment – from the laptop to the fridge to the toilet – to serve as a constant reminder of our work obligations. Of course, the line between sarcasm and practical advice is fuzzy here: you can laugh it off, or you can let it snap you back into productive mode. (kh)

Luiza Margan

Cache, 2023/24
Dekonstruierte Metallspinde, Handcreme; Maße variabel

Courtesy der Künstlerin

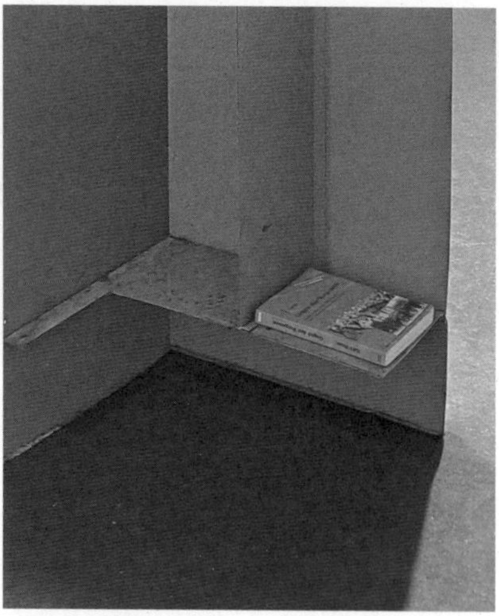

Cache ist eine Fortsetzung von Luiza Margans Beschäftigung mit den verschiedenen Formen der Arbeitsdarstellung, den Arbeitsbedingungen und dem Erbe der Arbeiterbewegung, deren historische Auswirkungen bis heute nachwirken. In ihren Installationen, Skulpturen, Filmen und Interventionen im öffentlichen Raum thematisiert die Künstlerin die Beziehung zwischen konkreter physischer Arbeit, der Arbeit von Kulturproduzent*innen und der immateriellen Erzeugung von Werten. Den Rahmen der Installation bilden drei Metallspinde, die dekonstruiert und wie Paravents aufgestellt sind, sodass – entgegen ihrer ursprünglichen Funktion – ihr Inhalt sichtbar ist. Die Schränke stehen stellvertretend für die Körper und Stunden von Arbeiter*innen, während der Titel auf einen geheimen Informationsspeicher verweist: Der Begriff „Cache" bezeichnet im Allgemeinen einen Zwischenspeicher, in dem Daten temporär gespeichert werden, um den Zugriff darauf zu beschleunigen und die Leistung zu verbessern.
Ursprünglich wurde die Installation für eine Ausstellung im Zeppelin-Museum in Friedrichshafen geschaffen und mit regionaler Zeitgeschichte angereichert. Für die Ausstellung im Kunsthaus Graz werden die dekonstruierten Schränke um eine ephemere Intervention erweitert. Drei mit Handcreme geschriebene Worte bringen auf den Punkt, wofür wir alle arbeiten: Lohn, Miete, Eigentum. Die weiche Creme, die im Laufe der Zeit vom harten, grob wirkenden Metall absorbiert wird und daher regelmäßig erneuert werden muss, verweist auf ständig wechselnde Arbeitsbedingungen und fügt der Installation zudem eine Geruchsebene hinzu. (kh)

Luiza Margan

Cache, 2023/24
Deconstructed metal lockers, hand cream; variable dimensions

Courtesy of the artist

Cache is a continuation of Luiza Margan's exploration of the various kinds of labour representation, working conditions and the legacy of the labour movement, whose historical impact can still be felt today. In her installations, sculptures, films and interventions in public space, the artist examines the relationship between concrete physical labour and the work of cultural producers and the immaterial production of value.
The frame of the installation is created by three metal lockers that have been deconstructed and set up as screens so that – contrary to their original function – their contents are visible. The lockers represent the bodies and hours of workers, while the title refers to a secret information store: the term 'cache' generally refers to a temporary storage area used to store data to increase the speed and performance of data access.
The installation was originally created for an exhibition at the Zeppelin Museum in Friedrichshafen and enhanced with regional contemporary history. For the exhibition at the Kunsthaus Graz, the deconstructed lockers are extended by an ephemeral intervention. Three words written in hand cream summarise what we all work for. Wages, rent, property. The soft cream, which over time is absorbed by the hard, coarse-looking metal and therefore needs to be renewed regularly, refers to the constantly changing working conditions and also adds a layer of smell to the installation. (kh)

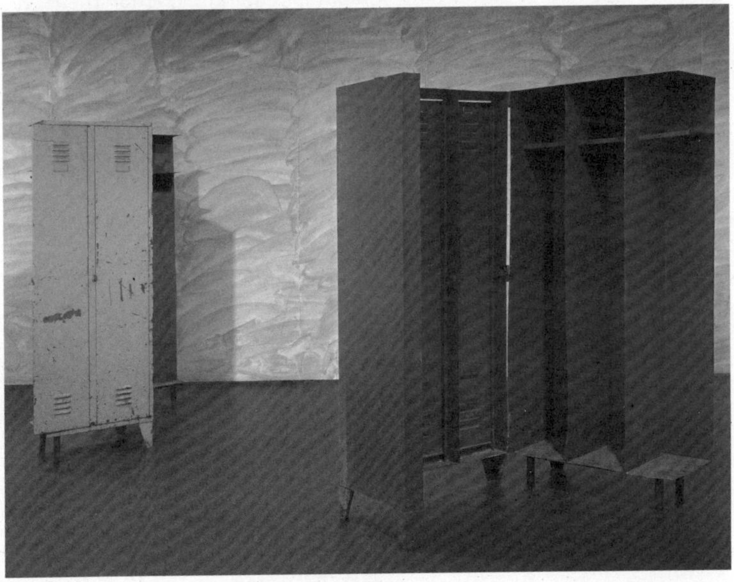

Pia Mayrwöger

Mischmaschine, 2021/2024
Mischmaschine, Leichtbeton, Wasser; Ø ca. 250 cm
Technische Umsetzung: Stefan Tiefengraber

Courtesy der Künstlerin

Maschinen sind funktionale bewegliche Objekte, die menschliche Arbeit erleichtern und einsparen sollen. Nicht zuletzt durch die rational-technische Optimierung ihrer Form faszinieren sie uns aber auch oft durch ihre Ästhetik. In der Betonmischmaschine wird Beton gemischt und, sobald das Mischverhältnis stimmt, die Trommel direkt vor Ort entleert. Dieser Vorgang wird so lange wiederholt, bis der Stück für Stück wachsende und aushärtende Betonkegel die Trommel in ihrer Beweglichkeit blockiert und die Maschine sich dadurch selbst außer Gefecht setzt. Sie verliert ihren Zweck und zurück bleibt ein rein ästhetisches Kunstobjekt.
In ihrer Auseinandersetzung mit verschiedenen Maschinen – die Künstlerin lässt auch Akkuschrauber funktionslos um den fest in der Wand verankerten Bohrer rotieren oder einen Bagger sich selbst ein- und dann wieder ausgraben – untersucht Pia Mayrwöger mit feinem Humor das arbeitsteilige Zusammenspiel von Menschen und Maschinen, sich verändernde Produktionsmethoden und Arbeitsabläufe.
Die unreflektierte, fast starrköpfige Wiederholung eines Arbeitsvorgangs konterkariert seinen ursprünglichen Zweck und stellt den Sinn von (gewissen) Arbeiten zur Diskussion. In einer Welt, in der von Menschen gesteuerte „klassische" Maschinen durch intelligente Roboter und selbstlernende KI-Systeme ersetzt werden, beginnt einem die sich selbst ihres Nutzens beraubende Mischmaschine beinahe leid zu tun. Pia Mayrwöger verleiht ihr einen fast schon menschlichen Charakter. (mg)

Pia Mayrwöger

Mischmaschine, 2021/2024
Concrete mixer, lightweight concrete, water; Ø approx. 250 cm
Technical realisation: Stefan Tiefengraber

Courtesy of the artist

Machines are functional moving objects designed to make human labour easier and to save time. In large part due to the rational and technical optimisation of their form, their aesthetics also often fascinate us. Concrete is mixed in the concrete mixer and, as soon as the mixing ratio is correct, the drum is emptied directly on site. This process is repeated until the concrete cone, gradually growing and hardening, blocks the drum's movement and the machine puts itself out of action. Its purpose is lost – all that remains is a purely aesthetic art object.
In her exploration of various machines – cordless screwdrivers rotating pointlessly around a drill fixed in a wall, or an excavator digging itself in and out again – Pia Mayrwöger uses subtle humour to investigate the work-sharing interplay between people and machines, changing production methods and work processes.
The unthinking, almost stubborn repetition of a work process defeats its original purpose and calls the meaningfulness of (certain) works into question. In a world where 'classic' machines controlled by humans are being replaced by intelligent robots and self-learning AI systems, we almost start to feel sorry for the mixer that destroys its own usefulness. Pia Mayrwöger allows it an almost human character. (mg)

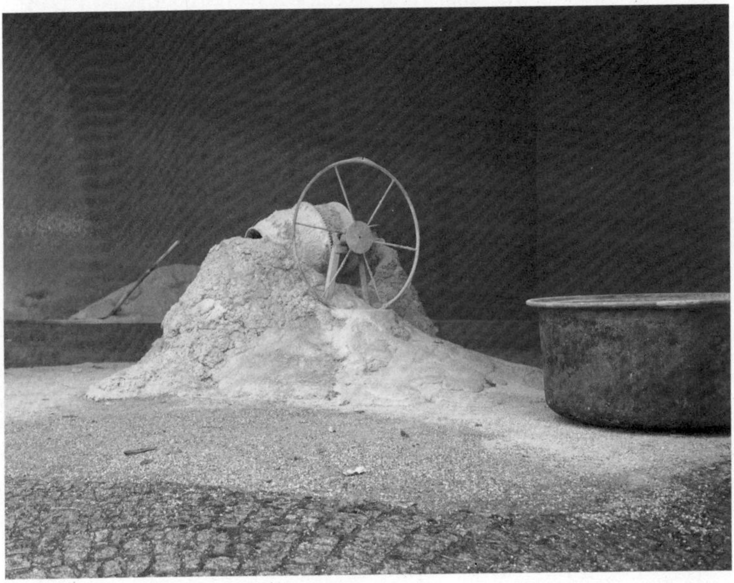

Sam Meech

Punchcard Economy: 8 Hours Labour, 2024
8 Stunden künstlerische Arbeit, repräsentiert durch Arbeitsvertrag, Arbeitstisch, Brother KH-830 Strickmaschine, Banner, Video; Maße variabel

Courtesy des Künstlers

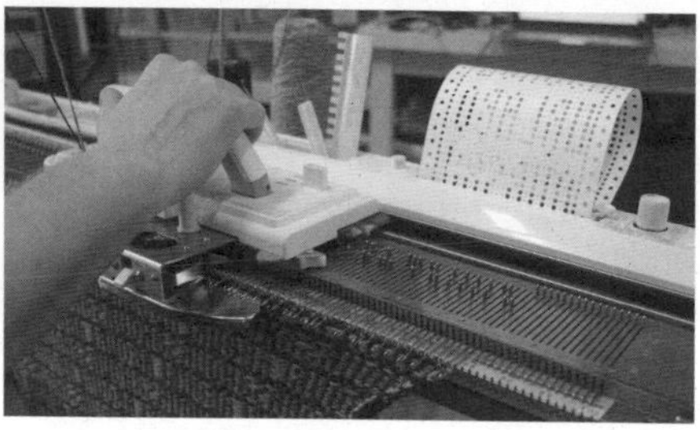

200 Jahre nachdem der britische Unternehmer und Sozialist Robert Owen die Bewegung für den Acht-Stunden-Tag ins Leben gerufen hat, erleben wir eine neue Ära der Arbeitswelt. Die digitale Technologie und die sich wandelnde Natur der Arbeit haben eine flexible, aber auch prekäre Wirtschaft geschaffen. Der traditionelle Begriff von „Arbeit" ist nicht länger an einen bestimmten Ort oder feste Zeiten gebunden. Die Arbeit ist in alle Bereiche unseres Lebens eingedrungen, und oft fällt es schwer zu definieren, was Arbeit ist und was nicht. New Work ist das Schlagwort der Stunde.
Punchcard Economy: 8 Hours Labour von Sam Meech ist eine künstlerische Reflexion über Owens Erbe und die gegenwärtige Realität. Durch ein maschinengestricktes Banner stellt der Künstler Überlegungen zur nordwestlichen Textilproduktion an und dokumentiert dabei gleichzeitig die Vielfalt moderner Arbeitsmuster. 2015 sammelte Meech zu diesem Zweck Daten von einer Vielzahl von Arbeitskräften, insbesondere aus den Bereichen Digitalisierung, Kreativwirtschaft und Kultur. Diese übertrug er auf die Lochkarten (Punchcards) der Strickmaschine und arbeitete sie in Form von unregelmäßigen Mustern ein. Seitdem arbeitet Meech weiter an diesem Konzept, wobei er die Lochkarte metaphorisch als Symbol für die digitale Entwicklung und die gleichzeitige Überwachung von Arbeits- und Zeitsystemen einsetzt.
Im Rahmen einer Performance im Kunsthaus Graz absolvierte Sam Meech einen symbolischen Acht-Stunden-Arbeitstag, inklusive einer halben Stunde Mittagspause. In Hemd und Anzughose, in Anspielung auf den Büroalltag vieler Menschen, strickte er vor Ort an einem Banner. Das Werk, das in der Ausstellung zu sehen ist, ist jedoch nicht das Textilstück (das zugegebenermaßen nach acht Stunden Arbeit eine beeindruckende Länge erreicht hat), sondern die Arbeit und die Zeit, die sie in Anspruch genommen hat. Ein zwischen der Kuratorin und dem Künstler abgeschlossener Arbeitsvertrag belegt, dass für die Performance ein angemessenes Künstler*innenhonorar nach den „Fair-Pay"-Richtlinien des Kulturrats Österreich bezahlt wurde. Dies unterstreicht die Transparenz und den Wert von Meechs künstlerischer Arbeit in einer Welt, in der die Grenzen zwischen Arbeit, Kunst und Leben zunehmend verschwimmen. (kh)

Sam Meech

Punchcard Economy: 8 Hours Labour, 2024
8 hours of art work, represented by work contract, work table, Brother KH-830 knitting machine, banner, video; variable dimensions

Courtesy of the artist

200 years after the British entrepreneur and socialist Robert Owen launched the movement for the eight-hour day, we are now witnessing a new era in the world of work. Digital technology and the changing nature of work have created a flexible yet also precarious economy. The traditional concept of 'work' is no longer tied to a particular place or fixed hours. Work has infiltrated all areas of our lives, and it is sometimes hard to define what is work and what is not. New Work is the buzzword of the hour.
Punchcard Economy: 8 Hours Labour by Sam Meech is an artistic reflection on Owen's legacy and the current reality. A machine-knitted banner addresses northwest textile production while at the same time documenting the diversity of modern labour patterns. In 2015, Meech collected data from a wide range of workers, especially from the areas of digitalisation, creative industries and culture. He transferred this to the punchcards of the knitting machine and incorporated it in the form of irregular patterns. Meech has since continued to work on this concept, employing the punchcard metaphorically as a symbol for digital development and the associated surveillance of labour and time systems.
As part of a performance at the Kunsthaus Graz Sam Meech completed a symbolic eight-hour working day, including a half-hour lunch break. Wearing a shirt and suit trousers, alluding to the everyday office life of many people, he knitted a banner on site. However, the work on display in the exhibition is not the textile piece (which admittedly reached an impressive length after eight hours of labour), but the work and the time it took. A work contract concluded between the curator and the artist proves that an appropriate artist's fee was paid for the performance in accordance with the 'Fair Pay' guidelines of the Austrian Cultural Council. This highlights the transparency and value of Meech's artistic work in a world where the boundaries between work, art and life are becoming increasingly blurred. (kh)

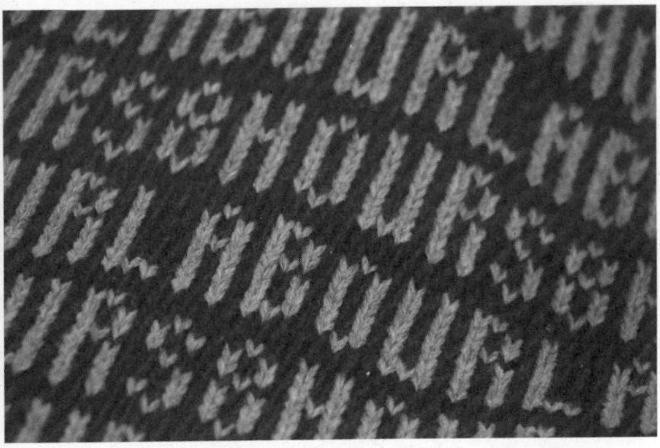

Michail Michailov

Just keep on going, 2015–fortlaufend
Videoinstallation bestehend aus derzeit 15 Videos; Loop
Kamera: Hannes Anderle

Courtesy des Künstlers

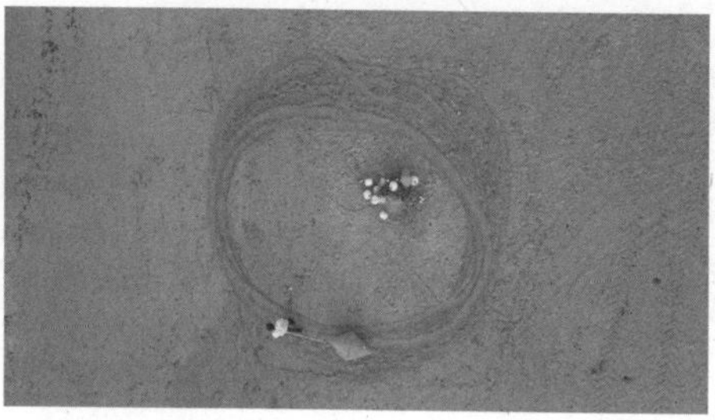

Michail Michailov beschäftigt sich mit dem Körper und dem Raum. Seine ständige Auseinandersetzung mit der Beziehung zwischen einer Form und ihrer Umgebung wendet sich grundlegenden Fragen der menschlichen Existenz und deren Bedingungen und Möglichkeiten zu.
Der Künstler erforscht diese existenziellen Themen in Zeichnungen, Videos und Performances und inszeniert dabei die vielen Variationen seines „Ichs". Immer wieder testet Michailov Architekturen und städtische Infrastrukturen, die ihn umgeben; die Orte, die er besucht, haben oft etwas Abgelegenes an sich. Wir sehen zum Beispiel Lagerräume auf der Rückseite von Gebäuden oder von Menschen genutzte Naturräume und – nur relativ klein als ein Element unter mehreren – den Künstler im immer gleichen weißen Schutzanzug. Die Farben, die Materialität, die Muster und die formalen Bedingungen der natürlichen oder urbanen Landschaften, in die sich Michailov mit immer neuen Körperkonfigurationen einschreibt, bezeugen die Existenz des Künstlers ebenso, wie sie seinen Körper verschwinden lassen.
Just keep on going legt den Schwerpunkt auf Wiederholungen ohne Anfang und Ende. Die Videos zeigen die Ausführung zyklischer Handlungen, deren Bedeutung in der Bewegung selbst und nicht im Endergebnis liegt. Sie zeigen die Interaktion des Künstlers mit einer fiktiven dystopischen Lebenswelt und sein ständiges Bemühen, diese zu meistern. Die Arbeit regt dazu an, über die Bedeutung von Wiederholung, Routine und dem Streben nach Sinnhaftigkeit in unserem täglichen Leben nachzudenken. So könnte die Videoserie als Metapher für die Wiederholung und den Zyklus des Arbeitslebens verstanden werden, wo oft die Bedeutung nicht im Endprodukt, sondern in der Handlung selbst liegt.
Die Suche nach Sinn, den nicht wenige von uns in ihrer Arbeit zu finden glauben, ist ein lebenslanger Prozess. Aber sich nur im Kreis zu drehen, ohne den geringsten Versuch, ihn zu durchbrechen, wäre für Michailov unbefriedigend. Runde für Runde führt uns der Künstler zu einer neuen Denkweise, zu neuen Wahrnehmungen und Erfahrungen, um uns der grundlegenden Frage zu stellen: Wer sind wir wirklich? (kh)

Michail Michailov

Just keep on going, 2015–ongoing
Video installation, currently consisting of 15 videos; loop
Camera: Hannes Anderle

Courtesy of the artist

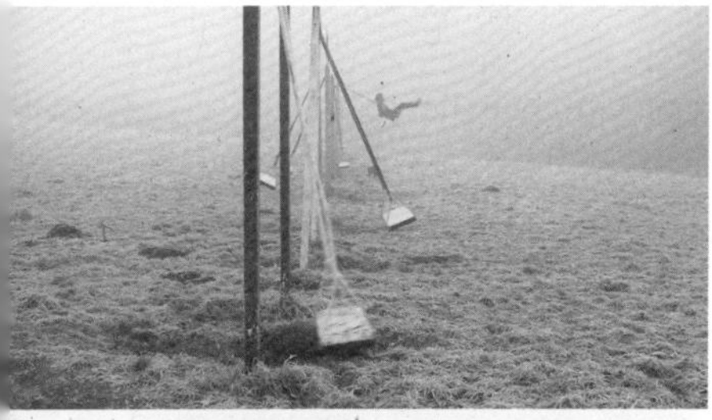

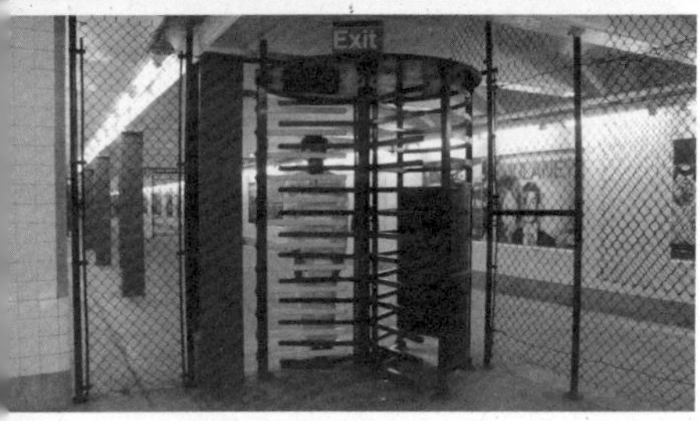

Michail Michailov's work examines the body and space. His constant exploration of the relationship between a form and its surroundings tackles the fundamental questions of human existence, its conditions and possibilities. The artist addresses these existential themes in drawings, videos and performances while staging the many variations of his 'self'. Again and again, Michailov tests the architecture and urban infrastructures that surround him in locations that often have something remote and secluded about them. We see storage rooms behind buildings or natural spaces used by people and – relatively small, as just one element among several – the artist appearing in the same white coverall. The colours, the materiality, the patterns and the formal conditions of the natural and urban landscapes in which Michailov is inscribed in ever new body configurations all testify to the existence of the artist while at the same time also making his body disappear.

Just keep on going focuses on repetitions with no beginning or end. The videos show the performance of cyclical actions whose meaning lies in the movement itself, and not in the end result. They show the artist's interaction with a fictitious dystopian world and his constant efforts to master it. The work prompts us to think about the importance of repetition, routine and the pursuit of meaningfulness in our daily lives. Hence the series could be seen as a metaphor for the repetition and cycle of working life, where often the meaning lies not in the end product but rather in the action itself.

The search for the meaning of life, which many of us believe we can find in our work, is a lifelong process. But going round in circles without even trying to break through would be unsatisfactory for Michailov. Round after round, the artist leads us towards a new way of thinking, to new perceptions and experiences so that we ask ourselves the fundamental question: Who are we, really? (kh)

Elisa Giardina Papa

Labor of Sleep, Have you been able to change your habits??, 2017
Installation; ca. 200 × 180 cm

Courtesy der Künstlerin und Galerie Tanja Wagner, Berlin
Im Auftrag des Whitney Museum of American Art

Elisa Giardina Papas Werke kommentieren die komplexen Dynamiken unserer zunehmend digitalisierten Welt. In multimedialen Installationen, Videos und Performances erforscht die Künstlerin die Auswirkungen der Technologie auf die Gesellschaft, oft mit einem kritischen und zum Nachdenken anregenden Ansatz. Zu den Themen, um die ihre Arbeiten kreisen, gehören digitale Überwachung und Online-Identität oder der Einfluss von Algorithmen auf unser tägliches Leben. Wie ist die Beziehung zwischen uns Menschen und den Maschinen, die uns die Arbeit „erleichtern", und wo liegen die Grenzen von Autonomie und Kontrolle im Bereich zwischen der digitalen und der physischen Welt? *Labor of Sleep, Have you been able to change your habits??* besteht aus einer Reihe kurzer Videoclips, die auf humorvolle Weise auf Selbstoptimierungs-Apps anspielen. Die Arbeit untersucht die Idee, dass Schlaf zu einem neuen Bereich geworden ist, in dem Verhaltens- und biologische Daten erfasst werden, um Schlafmuster zu optimieren. So wird die Zeit, die wir zum Ausruhen und Regenerieren nutzen, in eine Form von Arbeit umgewandelt, die der Datengewinnung gewidmet ist. Digitale Geräte dienen sowohl als Gift als auch als Heilmittel, indem sie die Zeit, die sie uns nehmen, wieder ausgleichen. Die täglichen Übungen und Bewertungen, die im Video vorgeschlagen werden, zeigen die Absurditäten der technologisch unterstützten Selbstoptimierung auf. Die Clips illustrieren, wie wir Technologien nutzen, um menschliche Schlafgewohnheiten innerhalb eines größeren Systems zu regulieren, das Menschen, Tiere und – nicht zuletzt – digitale Geräte umfasst. (kh)

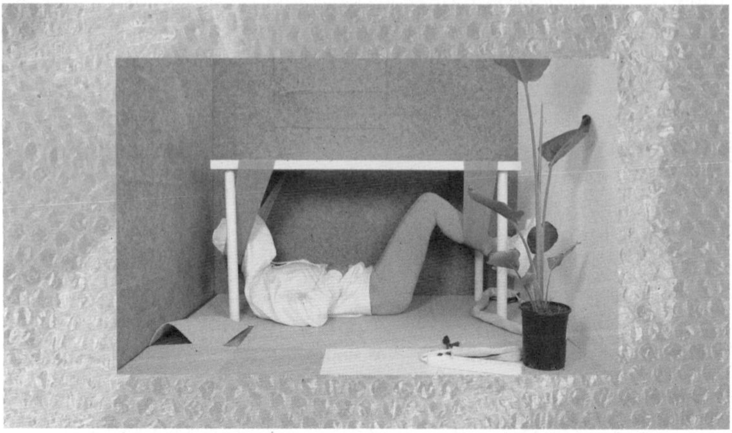

Elisa Giardina Papa

Labor of Sleep, Have you been able to change your habits??, 2017
Installation; approx. 200 × 180 cm

Courtesy of the artist and Galerie Tanja Wagner, Berlin
Commissioned by the Whitney Museum of American Art

Elisa Giardina Papa's work is a commentary on the complex dynamics of our increasingly digitalised world. Her multimedia installations, videos and performances explore the impact of technology on society, often taking a critical and thought-provoking approach. The themes around which her works revolve include digital surveillance, online identity and the influence of algorithms on our daily lives. What is the relationship between us humans and the machines that 'facilitate' our work, and where are the boundaries of autonomy and control in the area between the digital and physical worlds?
Labor of Sleep, Have you been able to change your habits?? consists of a series of short video clips that use humour to examine self-optimisation apps. The work investigates the idea that sleep has become a new area in which behavioural and biological data is collected in order to optimise sleep patterns. The time we take to rest and regenerate is transformed into a kind of labour devoted to data mining. Digital devices serve as both poison and cure by rebalancing the time they take away from us. The daily exercises and ratings suggested in the video demonstrate the absurdities of technology-supported self-optimisation. The clips illustrate how we use technology to regulate human sleep habits within a larger system that includes humans, animals and – not least – digital devices. (kh)

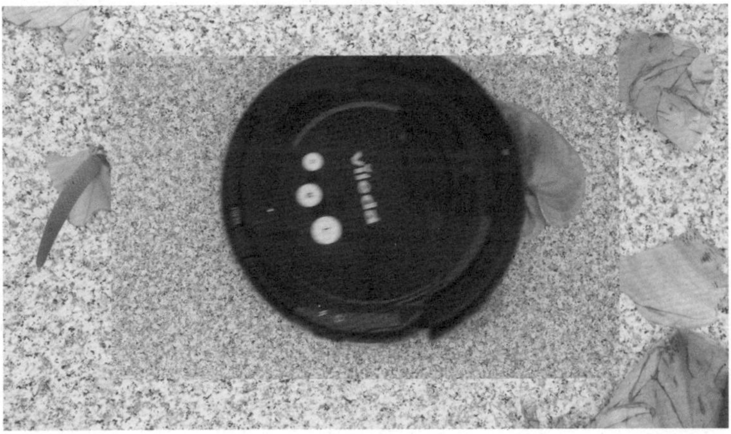

Nika Radić

Door – Gallery Cleaning, 2011
Video, SD; 4:17 min

Courtesy der Künstlerin

Nika Radić interessiert sich für zwischenmenschliche Beziehungen und die fragilen Grenzen zwischen öffentlicher und privater Sphäre. In verschiedenen Medien und künstlerischen Ausdrucksformen spielt sie mit Elementen des Alltäglichen und blickt unter die Oberfläche von vertrauten und gewöhnlichen Momenten und Verhaltensweisen.
Das Video *Door – Gallery Cleaning* zeigt eine „Putzfrau" (die Künstlerin selbst) bei der Reinigung eines fiktiven Raums hinter einer großen, herrschaftlich anmutenden Flügeltür, die in der Art eines Trompe-l'œil an die Wand „gemalt" ist. Durch den engen Bildausschnitt und das ständige Kommen und Gehen der Protagonistin lenkt der Film die Aufmerksamkeit auf verborgene, aber wesentliche Aktivitäten – unsichtbare Arbeit –, die normalerweise außerhalb der öffentlichen Wahrnehmung stattfinden, und bietet einen Einblick in den Galerie- oder Museumsraum außerhalb der Öffnungszeiten. Radićs Arbeit ist eine Auseinandersetzung mit dem sogenannten öffentlichen Raum und eine Reflexion über diejenigen, die von diesem Raum ausgeschlossen sind. Wer sind die Menschen, die hinter den Mauern der Gebäude in den Stadtzentren ihrer täglichen Arbeit nachgehen, sich dort aber kaum aufhalten, weil der sogenannte „öffentliche" Raum für sie zu teuer ist? Diejenigen, die hart arbeiten und dennoch von Armut betroffen sind – die sogenannten Working Poor? Lebensgroß an die Museumswand projiziert, vermittelt *Gallery Cleaning* einen Eindruck vom Leben der Menschen, die wir ständig sehen, aber oft nicht wahrnehmen. (kh)

Nika Radić

Door – Gallery Cleaning, 2011
Video, SD; 4:17 min

Courtesy of the artist

Nika Radić is interested in interpersonal relationships and the fragile boundaries that exist between the public and private spheres. In a range of media and artistic expressions she plays with elements of the everyday, looking beneath the surface of familiar and ordinary moments and behaviours.
The video *Door – Gallery Cleaning* shows a 'cleaning lady' (the artist herself) at work in a fictitious room behind a large, grand-looking double door that is 'painted' on the wall in the style of a trompe l'œil. The tight framing and the constant coming and going of the protagonist (actually the artist herself) draw attention to the hidden yet essential activities that usually take place outside of the public's perception – invisible work –, offering an insight into the gallery or museum space outside of opening hours. Radić's work is an examination of 'public space' and a reflection on those who are excluded from this space. Who are the people who go about their work every day behind the walls of city centre buildings but do not in fact spend much time there, because this so-called 'public' space is too expensive for them? Those who work hard and are still affected by poverty – the so-called working poor? As a life-size projection onto the museum wall, *Gallery Cleaning* gives an impression of the lives of the people we see all the time but often don't even notice. (kh)

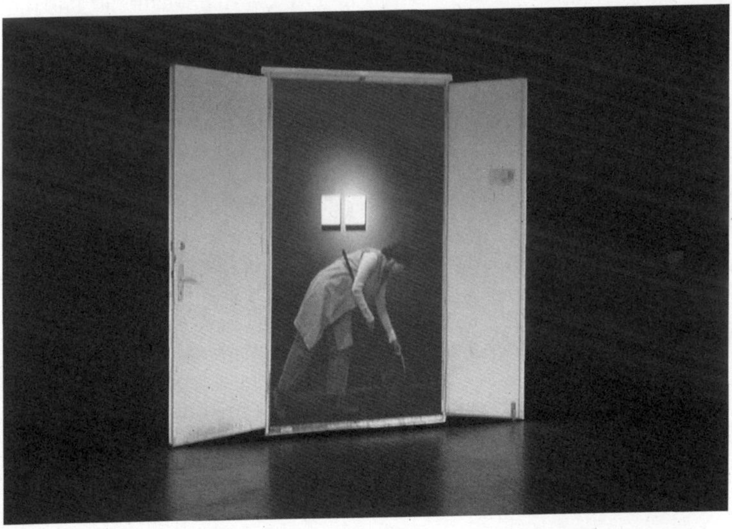

Martha Rosler

Semiotics of the Kitchen, 1975
Video; 6:18 min

Courtesy der Künstlerin, Electronic Arts Intermix (EAI), New York, und Galerie Nagel Draxler, Berlin/Köln/München

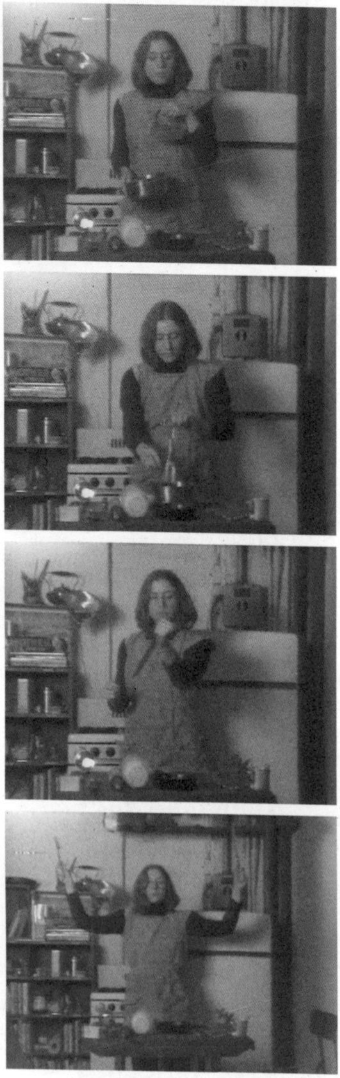

Das Küchen-ABC der Videokünstlerin Martha Rosler aus den 1970er-Jahren ist eine ikonische Arbeit feministischer Kunst. Im Mittelpunkt steht eine Frau (die Künstlerin selbst), die durch ihr Geschlecht, die Küche, die Schürze, die sie zu Beginn des Videos anzieht (a wie „apron“), und die Verwendung verschiedener Küchenutensilien alle typischen Zeichen bedient, die sie als „Hausfrau“ charakterisieren. Dem Alphabet folgend („bowl“, „chopper“, „dish“ ...), hält Rosler ein Küchenwerkzeug nach dem anderen in Händen, um den Gebrauch mit überspitzten, absurden und zum Teil aggressiv wirkenden Bewegungen zu imitieren. Nachdem sie dies bis zum Buchstaben U getan hat, nimmt Rosler ein Messer und eine Gabel und formt mit ihren Armen und ihrem Körper die letzten Buchstaben V, W, X und Y. Mit dem Messer schneidet sie schließlich mit einer Zorro-Geste durch die Luft, verschränkt die Arme vor dem Körper und schaut achselzuckend in die Kamera. Der Bildausschnitt und die frontal positionierte Protagonistin erinnern an eine Kochsendung im Fernsehen, wo – anders als in Millionen von Küchen in Privathaushalten – zu jener Zeit meist männliche Köche agierten und die Esskultur ganzer Nationen prägten.
Mit ihrer slapstickartigen Küchenshow nimmt Rosler die Auswirkungen der Hausarbeit auf die Rolle der Frau in der Gesellschaft ins Visier. Gleichzeitig stellt sie die Unzulänglichkeiten der Semiotik fest, jener Wissenschaft, die sich mit Zeichensystemen aller Art befasst und untersucht, was ein Zeichen sein kann und welche Funktionen es erfüllt. *Semiotics of the Kitchen* ist nicht zuletzt als feministische Botschaft an alle Frauen zu verstehen und beinhaltet jenes Hauptanliegen, das Martha Rosler in all ihren Werken antreibt: „Du kannst das!“ (kh)

Martha Rosler

Semiotics of the Kitchen, 1975
Video; 6:18 min

Courtesy of the artist, Electronic Arts Intermix (EAI), New York, and Galerie Nagel Draxler, Berlin/Cologne/Munich

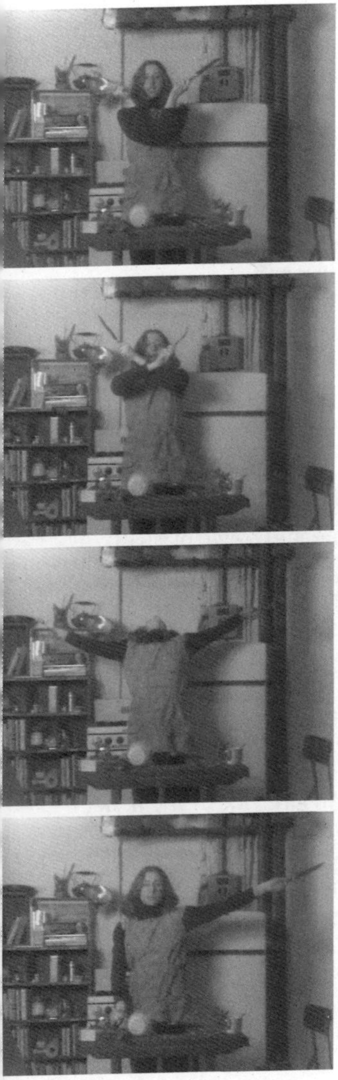

Video artist Martha Rosler's Kitchen ABC is an iconic work of feminist art from the 1970s. The video focuses on a woman (the artist herself) who displays all of the typical signs that mark her out as a 'housewife': her gender, the kitchen, the apron she puts on at the beginning (A for 'apron') and her use of various kitchen utensils. Running through the alphabet ('bowl', 'chopper', 'dish'...), Rosler holds up one utensil after another, miming their functions in absurd, exaggerated movements, sometimes with aggression. She carries on until she reaches the letter U, when she picks up a knife and fork and makes the shape of the letters V, W, X and Y with her arms and body. She finally takes the knife and cuts a Z through the air like Zorro, then folds her arms in front of her body and shrugs while looking at the camera. The framing and the protagonist facing the camera are reminiscent of a television cookery programme where – unlike the millions of kitchens in private homes – it was mostly male chefs who dominated the food culture of whole nations at that time.
With her slapstick-style kitchen show, Rosler targets the consequences of housework for the role of women in society. At the same time, she identifies the shortcomings of semiotics, the science that concerns sign systems of all kinds and examines what a sign can be and what functions it serves. *Semiotics of the Kitchen* is not least to be understood as a feminist message to all women and contains the main concern that drives Martha Rosler in all her works: 'You can do this!' (kh)

Sebastian Schmieg & Silvio Lorusso

Five Years of Captured Captchas, 2017
5 Leporellos, Schuber, Digitaldruck; insgesamt 25 × 9.064 cm

Courtesy der Künstler

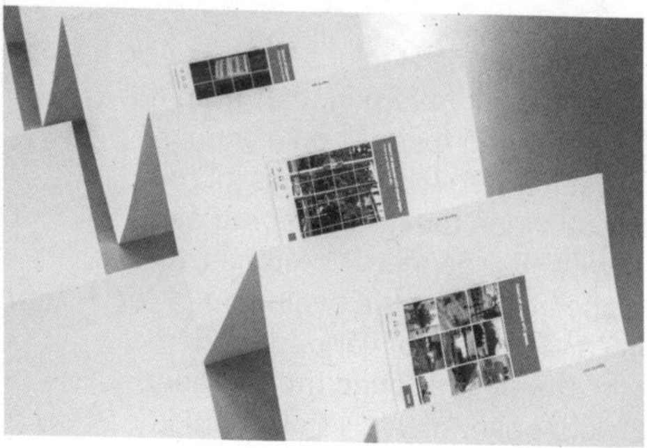

„☐ I'm not a robot" – „✓" – „Select all images with traffic lights." Wir alle kennen das und wer hat sich nicht schon darüber geärgert? So auch Silvio Lorusso und Sebastian Schmieg, die sich mit techno-sozialen Systemen und Plattformen beschäftigen, damit, wie diese unsere vernetzte Gesellschaft durchdringen und was hinter den digitalen Screens passiert. In fünf Leporellos haben sie jedes einzelne Captcha, das sie über fünf Jahre gelöst haben, abgebildet. Captchas (vollautomatische öffentliche Turing-Tests zur Unterscheidung von Computern und Menschen) sind die kleinen Muster- oder Bildtests, die wir im Internet immer wieder lösen müssen, um zu beweisen, dass wir keine Roboter sind. Sie dienen dazu, Webanwendungen vor Schäden durch missbräuchliche Eingaben durch Bots zu schützen. Doch diese Verifikation ist nicht die einzige Funktion von Captchas, vielleicht nicht einmal mehr ihre primäre.
In der chronologischen, über 90 Meter langen Anordnung der Screenshots beleuchten die Künstler die Entwicklung der Captchas – und damit auch die unbezahlte Mikroarbeit, die wir alle für den dahinterstehenden Konzern Google erledigen, wann immer wir eines lösen. Ging es zunächst um die Identifizierung verzerrter Buchstabenfolgen für das philanthropische Projekt der Digitalisierung von Büchern, die dann auf Google Books der Öffentlichkeit zur Verfügung gestellt werden, unterrichten wir nun Googles KI. Unentgeltlich bringen wir ihr bei, Autos von Schulbussen zu unterscheiden, Straßenschilder, Ampeln und Radfahrer*innen zu erkennen. Als Nicht-Roboter werden wir zu Werkzeugen einer nicht-menschlichen Intelligenz. Wegen des Crowdsourcings dieser Arbeit war Google 2016 sogar mit einer Sammelklage konfrontiert, die allerdings mit dem Argument abgelehnt wurde, der kurze Zeitaufwand, ein Captcha zu lösen, stelle keinen relevanten Arbeitsaufwand dar. Lorusso und Schmieg machen diese Arbeitsleistung sichtbar und thematisieren den Umgang mit Crowdsourcing durch einen globalen Konzern. *Five Years of Captured Captchas* kann in diesem Sinn auch als ein „feierlicher Fünfjahresbericht" der „fruchtbaren Zusammenarbeit" mit dem Konzern verstanden werden, wie es die Künstler in einer Mail an Google formulieren. (mg)

Sebastian Schmieg & Silvio Lorusso

Five Years of Captured Captchas, 2017
5 leporello books, slipcase, digital print; in total 25 × 9,064 cm

Courtesy of the artists

'☐ I'm not a robot' – '✓' – 'Select all images with traffic lights.' We have all experienced this – and who hasn't found it annoying? Silvio Lorusso and Sebastian Schmieg have, and investigate techno-social systems and platforms, how they permeate our networked society and what happens behind the digital screens. Every captcha they have solved over the course of five years is represented with a screenshot in five leporello books. Captchas (Completely Automated Public Turing Test to Tell Computers and Humans Apart) are the small pattern or image tests we need to solve over and again on the internet in order to prove that we are not robots. They serve to protect web apps from the damage caused by the entries of abusive bots. And yet this verification is not the only function of captchas, perhaps no longer even the primary function.

The chronological more than 90-metre-long array of screenshots traces the development of captchas – and so also the unpaid microwork that we all do for Google, the company behind most captchas, whenever we complete one. While initially we identified distorted sequences of letters for the philanthropic project of digitising books that were then made available to the public on Google Books, now we are instructing Google's AI. Free of charge, we are teaching it how to distinguish between cars and school buses and to recognise road signs, traffic lights and cyclists. As non-robots, we are becoming the tools of non-human intelligence. In 2016, Google even faced a class action lawsuit because of the crowdsourcing of this work. This was, however, rejected with the argument that the brief time required to solve a captcha did not constitute a relevant amount of work. Lorusso and Schmieg make this workload visible and raise the question of how we consider crowdsourcing used by a global corporation. In this sense, *Five Years of Captured Captchas* can also be seen as a 'quinquennial report' to 'celebrate our fruitful collaboration' with the company, as the artists wrote in their email to Google. (mg)

Sebastian Schmieg & Silvio Lorusso
2 Dec 2016 16:31:02 CET
To: captchas@google.com, work@google.com, collaboration@google.com, cognitive.resources@google.com, human.resources@google.com, humans@google.com, partners@google.com, info@google.com
Five Years of Captured Captchas

Dear Google,

today five years ago, while solving yet another CAPTCHA, we wondered how much time we invest in proving that we are humans and not robots. Since then, we have archived every single CAPTCHA that we passed.

We noticed that each time we are not just proving to be human but are in fact digitising books, deciphering house numbers, and training artificial intelligence. Most of this work over the years has been done for you.

We were never asked to join your workforce. Nonetheless, we proudly accepted the task to contribute our cognitive resources to help Google achieve its goals. Today after five years, we have collected 471 CAPTCHAs already.

Now, we are writing to present our quinquennial report which includes all the CAPTCHAs collected until now. We would be very happy to celebrate our fruitful collaboration, perhaps in your offices in Brussels or any other location you consider appropriate.

Thank you.

Best regards,

Silvio Lorusso & Sebastian Schmieg

Christoph Schwarz

Supercargo. Halbautomatisches Reisen, 2010
Video, HD; 13:30 min, chinesisch mit deutschen/englischen UT

Courtesy des Künstlers

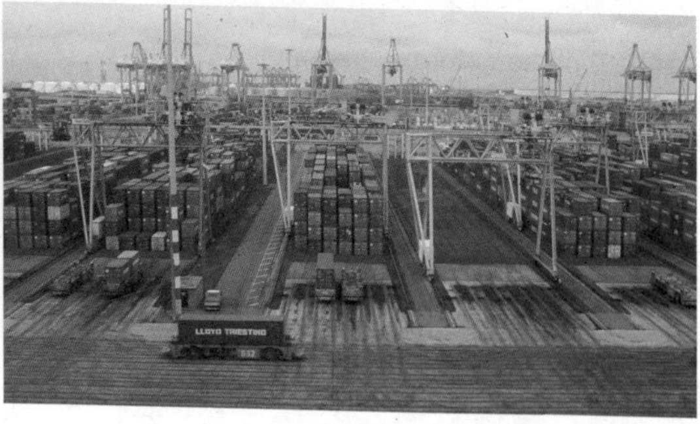

Christoph Schwarz wird zu einem Artist-in-Residence-Programm nach Shanghai eingeladen und entscheidet sich, an Bord eines Containerfrachters nach China zu reisen. Der künstlerische Selbsterfahrungstrip auf den Spuren des globalen Handels entwickelt sich zu einem existenzialistischen Erlebnis, das im mentalen Zusammenbruch des Künstlers gipfelt.
Die vielbefahrene Route Hamburg/Rotterdam–Shanghai widerspiegelt das ungleiche Verhältnis im wirtschaftlichen Austausch zwischen dem konsumierenden Kontinent Europa und China, der „Werkbank der Welt". In diese Richtung werden nur wenige Waren transportiert, sondern vor allem nichtmaterielle Güter wie Wissen und Kultur – im Film personifiziert durch Schwarz. So sind die bunten Container, die sich als stille Protagonisten durch den ganzen Film ziehen, großteils leer. Die normierten, 3 × 3 × 6 Meter großen Metallkisten stehen nicht nur für die logistischen Aspekte des Welthandels, sondern auch für seine weitreichenden Auswirkungen, komplexen geopolitischen Zusammenhänge und die sozialen Ungerechtigkeiten, die er auslöst, verstärkt und verfestigt. Sie machen die Dimension und Wirkungsmacht der Globalisierung überhaupt erst abbildbar.
Zunächst hochmotiviert („Ich stelle mir dabei vor, ich hätte mit dem Aufwischen im Maschinenraum eine tragende Rolle in der Weltwirtschaft") entwickelt Schwarz in der sozialen Isolation an Bord persönliche Beziehungen zu den Containern, als wären sie Freunde. Das schrittweise Entstehen dieser Extremsituation wird durch einen minimalen Eingriff des Filmemachers ermöglicht, der zu Beginn schildert, er sei der einzige Mensch an Bord des „halbautomatischen" Superfrachters MS Confidence. Nur aus versicherungstechnischen Gründen müsse ein menschliches Wesen an Bord sein, der Rest laufe ferngesteuert. Diese vielleicht prophetische Abweichung von der Realität eröffnet eine neue Bedeutungsebene und lässt uns voller Vertrauen tief in die humorvoll-essayistisch erzählte Verschränkung seiner individuellen Situation – inklusive der Reflexion künstlerischer Arbeit – mit den globalen Ungleichheiten der übermächtigen wirtschaftlichen Vernetzungen eintauchen. (mg)

Christoph Schwarz

Supercargo. Halbautomatisches Reisen, 2010
Video, HD; 13:30 min, Chinese with English/German subtitles

Courtesy of the artist

Christoph Schwarz is invited to Shanghai on an artist-in-residence programme and decides to travel to China on board a container freighter. His artistic journey of self-awareness on the trail of global trade evolves into an existentialist experience that culminates in a mental breakdown.
The busy Hamburg/Rotterdam-Shanghai route reflects the unequal relationship in economic exchange between the consuming continent of Europe and the 'workbench of the world', China. Little merchandise is transported in this direction, instead it is chiefly a flow of non-material goods like knowledge and culture – as personified by Schwarz in his film. The vibrant containers featured as the silent protagonists throughout *Supercargo* are mostly empty. The standardised 3 × 3 × 6 metre metal crates have become iconic symbols not just for the logistical aspects of global trade, but also for its far-reaching consequences, complex geopolitical contexts and the social injustices that it causes, reinforces and consolidates. They make the dimensions and impact of globalisation somehow mappable and tangible.
Initially highly motivated *('I would imagine that my swirling wiping motions in the engine room were major contributions to the inner-workings of the global economy')*, in his social isolation Schwarz establishes personal relationships with the containers, as if they were friends. The gradual development of this extreme situation is facilitated with a minimal intervention by the filmmaker, who at the beginning explains that he is the only person on board the 'semi-automatic' super freighter MS Confidence. A human being must be on board purely for insurance reasons, otherwise everything is remote-controlled. This perhaps prophetic detachment from reality opens up a new level of meaning and allows us to immerse ourselves with trust in the humorous essayistic narrative that interweaves his individual situation – including reflection on an artist's work – with the global inequality of powerful economic networks. (mg)

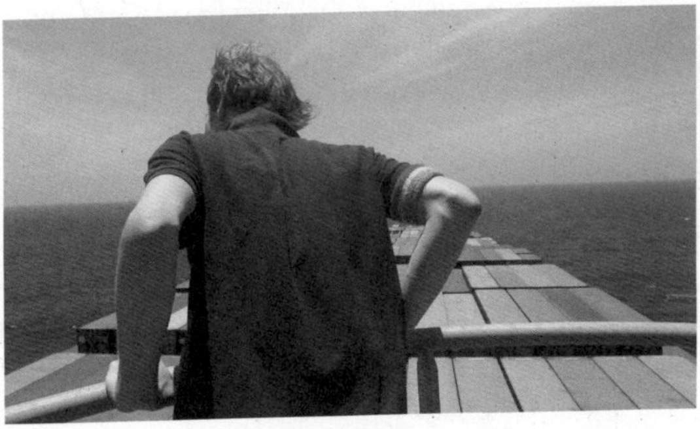

Selma Selman

AEG Vampyr 1400, 2017
Dokumentation der Performance im acb Attachment, Budapest
Video; 9:46 min, Staubsauger

Courtesy der Künstlerin und acb gallery, Budapest

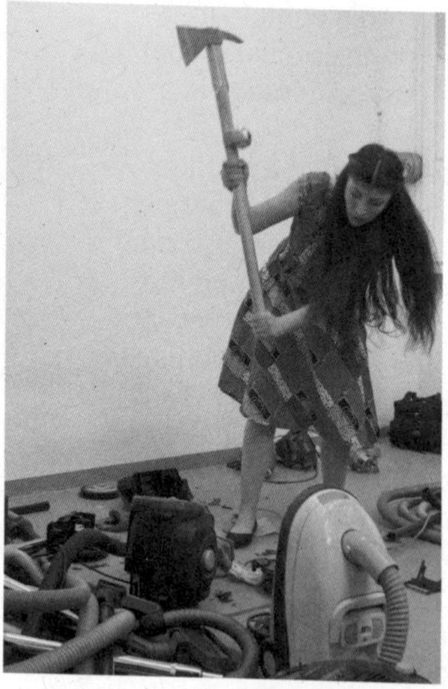

Eine junge Frau in einem roten Sommerkleid zerstört mit einer Axt einhundert Staubsauger. Sie tut das mit vollem Körpereinsatz, aber auch mit professioneller Routine. Und in der dafür unüblichen Umgebung einer Kunstgalerie.
In der kraftvollen Performance *AEG Vampyr 1400* adressiert Selma Selman schonungslos gesellschaftliche Hierarchien und mehrfache rassistische und geschlechtsspezifische Diskriminierungen, Spannungen und Traumata.
Wie viele ihrer Arbeiten nimmt diese Performance ihren Ausgangspunkt in Selmans persönlicher Biografie als Künstlerin mit Romnja-Hintergrund und überträgt sie in kritische und gesellschaftspolitisch engagierte Praxis. Aus der persönlichen Erzählung erwächst eine Reflexion über kollektive Identität, das auferlegte soziale Umfeld, über die entgegengebrachte Wahrnehmung und das Streben nach Selbstbestimmung.
Die Zerstörung der Staubsauger, als Haushaltsgerät auch Symbol für die meist von Frauen unbezahlt und unsichtbar in der privaten Sphäre des Haushalts geleistete Arbeit, ist ein radikaler Akt der Befreiung aus einer von patriarchalen Rollenbildern und sozialer Ungerechtigkeit bestimmten Lebensrealität.
Die Zerstörung – oder Zerlegung – der Staubsauger bezieht sich aber ebenso auf eine weitere wesentliche Ebene in Selmans Werk: Die Sammlung wertvoller Metalle, ihre Gewinnung aus ausrangierten Geräten und Autos und deren Verkauf an Altmetallhändler*innen ist die Lebensgrundlage vieler Vertreter*innen der Roma wie auch anderer marginalisierter gesellschaftlicher Gruppen. So auch Selmans eigener Familie, die bei vielen ihrer Performances mitwirkt. Selmans Performance transferiert diese alltägliche (Überlebens-)Praxis informeller Ökonomie in den Kontext künstlerischer Arbeit. Sie spricht damit Fragen der Wertschöpfung und des Umgangs mit Ressourcen – Tausende Roma betrieben Urban Mining, schon lange bevor es der Begriff in den akademischen Nachhaltigkeitsdiskurs schaffte – ebenso an wie solche der Wertschätzung, Repräsentation und der Konstruktion von Identität. Bei Selma Selman wird der performative Akt zur physischen Arbeit. Oder ist es umgekehrt? (mg)

Selma Selman

AEG Vampyr 1400, 2017
Documentation of the performance at acb Attachment, Budapest
Video; 9:46 min, vacuum cleaners

Courtesy of the artist and acb gallery, Budapest

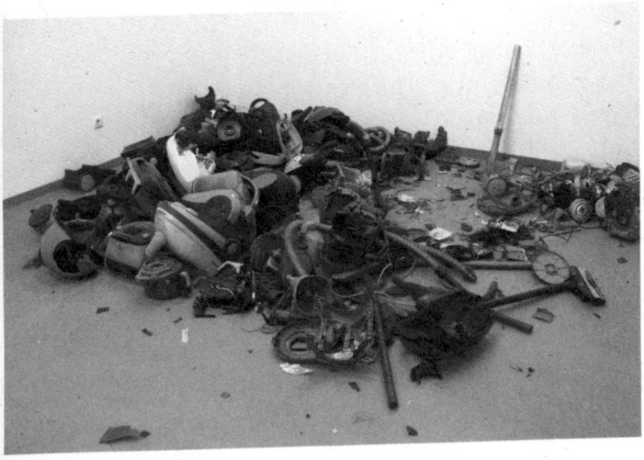

A young woman in a red summer dress destroys one hundred vacuum cleaners with an axe. She does this using her full physical force, but also with a sense of professional routine. And in the unusual setting of an art gallery. In the powerful performance *AEG Vampyr 1400*, Selma Selman starkly addresses societal hierarchies and multiple racial and gender-specific discriminations, tensions and traumas.
Like many of her works, the performance draws on Selman's personal biography as an artist from a Roma background, translating this into critical and socio-politically engaged practice. The personal narrative gives rise to a reflection on collective identity, the social environment imposed on us, the perception we are accorded and the pursuit of self-determination.
Vacuum cleaners are household appliances that also symbolise the unpaid and invisible work usually performed by women in the private sphere of the household. Hence their destruction is a radical act of liberation from a life reality determined by patriarchal gender roles and social injustice.
The demolishing – or dismantling – of the devices also refers to another important level of Selman's work: collecting valuable metals, extracting them from discarded appliances and cars and selling them to scrap metal dealers constitutes the livelihood of many Roma as well as other marginalised social groups. This includes Selman's own family, who participate in many of her performances. Selman's performance transfers this everyday (survival) practice of informal economy into the context of artistic work. She thereby addresses issues of value and the use of resources – thousands of Roma were already practising urban mining long before the term became current in the academic discourse on sustainability – as well as those of appreciation, representation and the construction of identity. In Selma Selman's work, the performative act becomes physical labour. Or is it the other way around? (mg)

Santiago Sierra

Repetition of the writing of a phrase, Kunsthaus Graz, Austria. May/July/September 2024, 2024
Performance

Courtesy des Künstlers
In Kooperation mit ISOP – Innovative Sozialprojekte

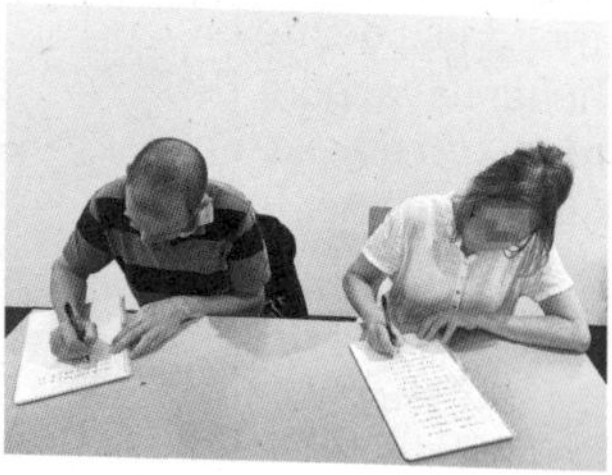

Für seine erste große Einzelausstellung in Europa, die im Jahr 2000 im KW Institute for Contemporary Art in Berlin stattfand, rekrutierte der Künstler Santiago Sierra sechs Asylwerber*innen in städtischen Asylunterkünften, die gegen Entlohnung während der knapp sechswöchigen Ausstellungsdauer für jeweils vier Stunden täglich und an sechs Tagen der Woche auf einem Stuhl unter einem Pappkarton sitzen sollten. *Workers who cannot be paid, remunerated to remain inside cardboard boxes* wurde an zwei weiteren Orten – etwa zeitgleich in Guatemala City und später in New York – unter leicht veränderten Bedingungen und Titeln realisiert und markiert einen Höhepunkt in Sierras provokanter und politisch aufgeladener Kunstarbeit.
Sierras Interesse gilt sozialen und ökonomischen Fragen, die Machtstrukturen, Ungleichheiten und Ausbeutung betreffen. Ein zentrales Thema in Sierras Werk ist die Arbeitswelt, konkret Arbeitsmigration und die Ausbeutung von Arbeiter*innen. Seine Zurschaustellung von Menschen in extremen oder erniedrigenden Situationen lenkt die Aufmerksamkeit auf die prekären Arbeits- und Lebensbedingungen vieler Gesellschaftsschichten – seien es nun Asylwerber*innen, Menschen migrantischer Herkunft oder Arbeitslose. Die oft schockierende und kontroversiell betrachtete Konfrontation von Kunstpublikum mit Menschen aus vulnerablen Gruppen in seinen Aktionen und Performances zielt darauf ab, gesellschaftliche Tabus zu brechen und ein Bewusstsein für politische und soziale Ungerechtigkeiten zu schaffen. Ursprünglich als Reaktion auf die weltweit geführte Debatte rund um die Gesundheitskontrollen anlässlich der Corona-Pandemie, realisierte Sierra 2022 die Performance *Repetition of the writing of a phrase* in Barcelona, in der er zwei Langzeitarbeitslose über Stunden den immer gleichen Satz „My body does not belong to me" auf A4-Bögen schreiben ließ. Santiago Sierra hat diese Arbeit für das Kunsthaus Graz leicht adaptiert: Hier fanden an drei Tagen ähnliche Performances statt, bei denen zwei Menschen mit Migrationshintergrund immer wieder den Satz „Ich werde niemals einem Europäer / einer Europäerin die Arbeit wegnehmen" zu Papier brachten. Die anschließende Rahmung und Hängung dieses Bekenntnisses, die einem strengen Raster folgt, spielt auf die bedeutende Konzeptkünstlerin Hanne Darboven an, die ihre akribischen, detaillierten Notizen auf Millimeterpapier in dichten Anordnungen zu raumgreifenden Installationen arrangierte. (kh)

Santiago Sierra

Repetition of the writing of a phrase, Kunsthaus Graz, Austria. May/July/September 2024, 2024
Performance

Courtesy of the artist
In cooperation with ISOP – Innovative Sozialprojekte

For his first major solo exhibition in Europe, at the KW Institute for Contemporary Art in Berlin in 2000, the artist Santiago Sierra recruited six asylum seekers from city refugee centres. In exchange for payment they were to sit on a chair under a cardboard box for four hours a day, six days a week, over the almost six weeks of the exhibition. *Workers who cannot be paid, remunerated to remain inside cardboard boxes* was realised at two further locations – around the same time in Guatemala City and later in New York – with slightly different conditions and titles, marking a high point in Sierra's provocative and politically charged work.
Sierra's interest lies in social and economic issues related to power structures, inequalities and exploitation. A central theme in Sierra's work is the world of labour, to be precise, labour migration and the exploitation of workers. By displaying people in extreme or degrading situations he draws attention to the precarious working and living conditions of many social strata – whether they are asylum seekers, people from a migration background or the unemployed. His often shocking and controversial confrontation of an art audience with people from vulnerable groups in his actions and performances aims to break social taboos and raise awareness of political and social injustices. Originally as a reaction to the worldwide debate around health checks during the pandemic, in 2022 Sierra staged the performance *Repetition of the writing of a phrase* in Barcelona, in which he asked two long-term unemployed people to write the sentence 'My body does not belong to me' on A4 paper for hours on end. Santiago Sierra has slightly adapted this work for the Kunsthaus Graz. Similar performances happened here on three days, during which two people with a migration background repeatedly wrote the sentence 'I will never steal a job from a European' on paper. The subsequent framing and hanging of this declaration, which follows a strict grid, references the work of prominent conceptual artist Hanne Darboven, who set out her meticulous, detailed notes on graph paper in dense arrangements creating expansive installations. (kh)

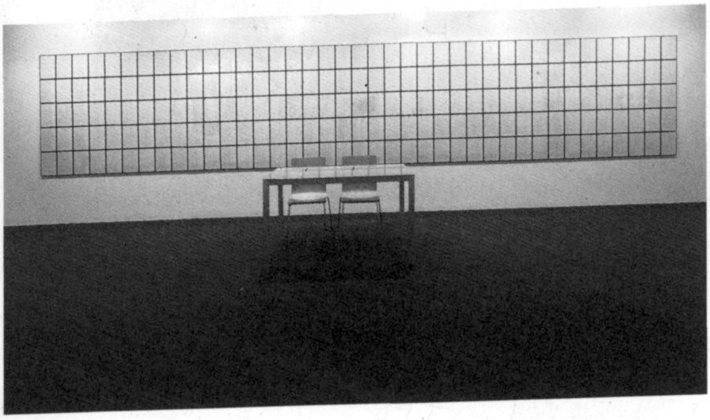

Lia Sudermann & Simon Nagy

Kein Wunder, 2024
Video; 11:26 min

Courtesy der Künstler*innen
In Kooperation mit dem Museum für Geschichte, Universalmuseum Joanneum

Kein Wunder ist der zweite gemeinsame Film von Lia Sudermann und Simon Nagy. Der Beginn ihrer Zusammenarbeit fiel mit dem ersten Covid-Lockdown zusammen, bei dem sich beide in einer intensiven Betreuungsbeziehung und entsprechender Isolation befanden. In dieser Situation begannen Sudermann und Nagy, sich gegenseitig Sprachnachrichten zu schicken, die später das Voiceover für ihren filmischen Essay *Invisible Hands* (2021) bildeten – eine Arbeit, die ein sensibles, humorvolles Porträt der Sorgearbeit in der Familie zeichnet und aus geschnittenem Material von Amateurinnenvideos besteht. Auch die aktuelle Arbeit *Kein Wunder* beleuchtet einige widersprüchliche Dimensionen im Dialog mit Archivmaterial: Die Ausstellung *Alles Arbeit. Frauen zwischen Erwerbs- und Sorgetätigkeit, Fotoarchiv Blaschka 1950–1966* im Museum für Geschichte untersucht den gesellschaftlichen Blick auf weibliche Arbeit und fragt, welche Formen von Arbeit fotografiert wurden – und welche unsichtbar bleiben. Anhand der Kontaktbögen aus dem Fotoarchiv Blaschka spinnen Sudermann und Nagy ähnlich wie bei *Invisible Hands* in einem dialogischen Voicemail-Austausch ihre persönlichen Assoziationen zu Doppelbelastung und Hausfrauendasein und teilen ihre Gedanken über eine Gesellschaft, in der Frauen hierzulande im Durchschnitt noch immer 18,5 % weniger pro Stunde verdienen als Männer und fast doppelt so viel unbezahlte Sorgearbeit leisten. (kh)

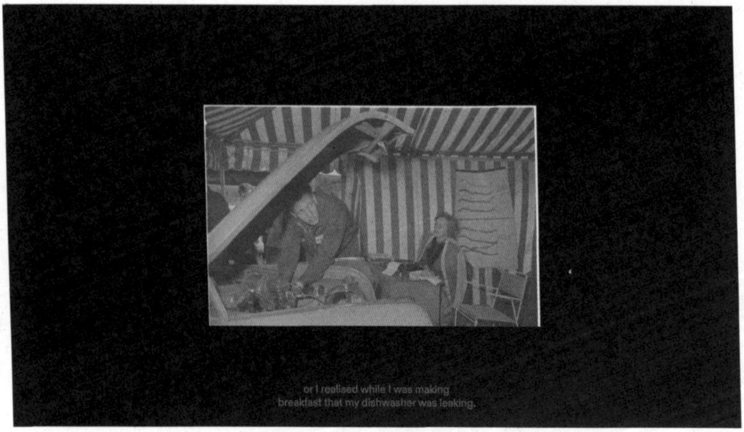

Lia Sudermann & Simon Nagy

No wonder, 2024
Video; 11:26 min

Courtesy of the artists
In cooperation with the History Museum, Universalmuseum Joanneum

No wonder is the second film Lia Sudermann and Simon Nagy have made together. The beginning of their collaboration coincided with the first COVID lockdown, during which both artists found themselves in an intense care relationship and corresponding isolation. In this situation Sudermann and Nagy began sending each other voice messages, which later became the voiceover for their film essay *Invisible Hands* (2021) – a work that draws a sensitive, humorous portrait of care work in the family and is made up of edited material from amateur videos.
No wonder also sheds light on some contradictory dimensions in dialogue with archive material: The exhibition *All work. Women between Paid Employment and Care Work, Fotoarchiv Blaschka 1950–1966* at the History Museum examines society's view of women's labour and asks what kinds of work were photographed – and which remain invisible. Using the contact sheets from the Blaschka photo archive, Sudermann and Nagy weave their personal associations around the double burden and being a housewife into a dialogue-like voicemail exchange, similar to *Invisible Hands,* and share their thoughts on a society in which women in this country still earn on average 18.5% less per hour than men and do almost twice as much unpaid care work. (kh)

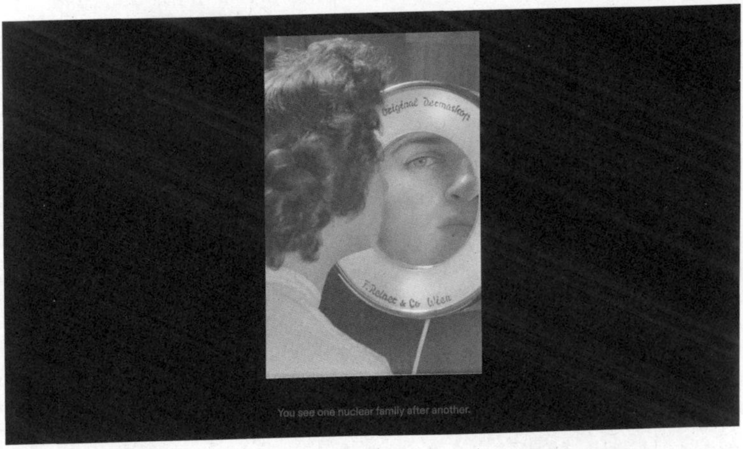

Oliver Walker

One Euro, 2015
Sechs-Kanal-Videoinstallation;
1:03 h, 29 min, 9:50 min, 3:17 min, 0:49 min, 0:01 min

Courtesy des Künstlers
Unterstützt von Arts Council England

In Oliver Walkers Videoinstallation *One Euro* ist auf sechs Monitoren je eine Person in verschiedenen Teilen der Welt bei der Arbeit zu beobachten. Jedes Video dauert so lange, wie die jeweilige Person braucht, um den Gegenwert von einem Euro zu verdienen. Dementsprechend variieren die Filmlängen von mehr als einer Stunde für schlecht bezahlte Arbeit in der Landwirtschaft im globalen Süden über etwas besser bezahlte Industriejobs und Tätigkeiten für ein mittleres Einkommen und reichen bis zu einer Sekunde, die ein CEO des globalen Nordens im Bild verweilt. Die erschütternden Ungleichheiten werden für die Betrachter*innen dadurch deutlich, dass ein Teil der Monitore die meiste Zeit schwarz bleibt, während andere Bildschirme im Dauerbetrieb sind. Ein Paradoxon, wenn man bedenkt, dass die Arbeit genau jener Menschen, die am härtesten für ihr Geld zu arbeiten haben, meist unsichtbar bleibt.
Walker nutzt die Zeit, um das Verhältnis zwischen Arbeit und Geld in ein subjektiveres Medium zu übertragen. Der Ausspruch „Zeit ist Geld" stammt von Benjamin Franklin und erschien erstmals 1748 in dessen Buch *Advice to Young Merchants* (Ratschläge für junge Kaufleute). Ursprünglich bezog sich dieser Satz auf die Arbeit und die Bedeutung von Effizienz und Produktivität, doch in seiner heutiger Anwendung betont er die kostbare und begrenzte Natur der Zeit, indem er ihren Wert mit dem finanziellen Konzept des Geldes verknüpft. Oliver Walkers Videoinstallation macht deutlich, dass nicht nur das Geld, sondern auch die verfügbare Zeit ungerecht verteilt ist – je nachdem, wie viel Arbeit wir für unser Geld leisten müssen und mit welchen Privilegien wir aufgrund unserer Herkunft ausgestattet sind. (kh)

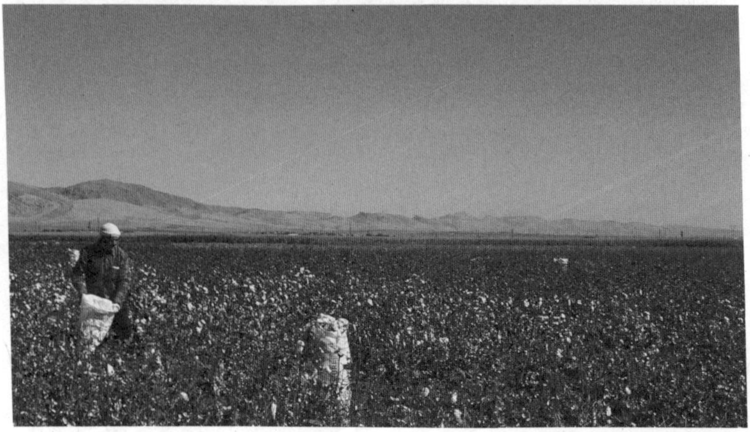

Oliver Walker

One Euro, 2015
Six-channel video installation;
1:03 h, 29 min, 9:50 min, 3:17 min, 0:49 min, 0:01 min

Courtesy of the artist
Supported by Arts Council England

In Oliver Walker's video installation *One Euro,* six monitors each show a person at work in different parts of the world. Each video lasts as long as it takes the person in question to earn the equivalent of one euro. As a result, the films vary in length from more than one hour for low-paid agricultural work in the global south to slightly better paid industrial jobs and middle-income jobs, and range up to one second, the time a CEO from the global north remains on the screen. The shocking inequalities are highlighted for viewers in that some of the screens remain black for most of the time, whereas others run continuously. A paradox, if one considers that the labour of those who have to work hardest for their money usually remains invisible.
Walker uses time to translate the relationship between labour and money into a more subjective medium. The phrase 'time is money' was coined by Benjamin Franklin and first appeared in 1748 in his book *Advice to Young Merchants*. Although it originally referred to work and the importance of efficiency and productivity, in its modern context it asserts the precious and limited nature of time by tying its value to the financial concept of money. Oliver Walker's video installation illustrates that it is not only money that is unfairly distributed, but also the time we have available – depending on how much work we have to do for our money and the privileges we possess because of our backgrounds. (kh)

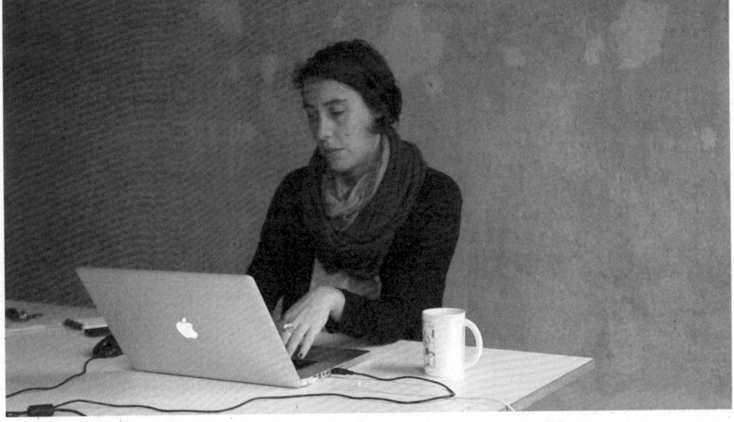

Glossar

24/7
24 Stunden, 7 Tage die Woche – also rund um die Uhr. Die in den 1980er-Jahren in den USA geprägte Abkürzung hat sich mit der Entwicklung moderner Kommunikationsmittel und der damit verbundenen ständigen Verfügbarkeit von Waren und Dienstleistungen immer weiter verbreitet. Inzwischen wird 24/7 auch mit ständiger Erreichbarkeit assoziiert, z. B. im Zusammenhang mit Kundenservice – ein Marketingschlagwort, das suggerieren soll, immer verfügbar zu sein. Damit steht 24/7 auch für Schichtbetrieb.

Acht-Stunden-Tag
Mit dem Slogan „8 hours labour, 8 hours recreation, 8 hours rest" (8 Stunden Arbeit, 8 Stunden Erholung, 8 Stunden Freizeit) leitete der walisische Unternehmer und Sozialreformer Robert Owen den Kampf um die Verkürzung der Arbeitszeit und Verbesserung der Arbeitsbedingungen ein, der von der ab den 1830ern erstarkenden → Gewerkschaftsbewegung in Großbritannien geführt wurde. In Österreich wurde der Acht-Stunden-Tag nach Ende des Ersten Weltkriegs eingeführt. Ab Jänner 1919 galt er für alle Beschäftigten in privaten und öffentlichen Betrieben – mit Ausnahmen wie der Landwirtschaft.

Arbeiterbewegung
In der Zeit der Industrialisierung zu Beginn des 19. Jahrhunderts bildete sich eine neue verarmte Unterschicht – die „arbeitende Classe". Armut und Elend entluden sich häufig in Unruhen. Bald bildeten sich solidarische Zusammenschlüsse. Ab den 1830er-Jahren kam es zu organisierten Protesten für bessere Arbeitsbedingungen, gerechtere Löhne und die Anerkennung von → Gewerkschaften. Während der Revolution von 1848, die großen Einfluss auf die Arbeiterbewegung hatte, wurden wesentliche Grundlagen für die Verkürzung der Arbeitszeit (10-Stunden-Tag) und Lohnerhöhungen gelegt.

Arbeiterklasse
→ Arbeiterbewegung

Arbeitslos
Trotz Wirtschaftskrise verzeichnet Österreich vergleichsweise niedrige Arbeitslosenzahlen (Stand März 2024: 291.468 Personen, Quelle: AMS), dazu melden viele Branchen einen Arbeitskräftemangel. Dennoch ist zwischen den politischen Parteien eine Debatte über mögliche Kürzungen des Arbeitslosengeldes oder die Einführung eines degressiven Modells wie in Dänemark oder Schweden entbrannt. Derzeit beträgt die Nettoersatzrate für Arbeitslose 55 % des letzten Monatsgehalts für 20 bis 52 Wochen, danach 51 % Notstandshilfe. Damit hat Österreich bereits jetzt eine der niedrigsten Nettoersatzraten in Europa. Personen mit geringer Bildung und Migrationshintergrund sind stärker von Arbeitslosigkeit betroffen, ebenso steigt die Jugendarbeitslosigkeit. Die Langzeitarbeitslosenquote hat sich heute im Vergleich zu vor zehn Jahren fast verdoppelt.

Arbeitskampf
→ Streik

Arbeitsmigration
Arbeitsmigration, auch Erwerbsmigration genannt, bezieht sich auf Wanderungen, die primär der Aufnahme oder dem Wechsel einer Erwerbstätigkeit dienen. Arbeitsmigrant*innen der ersten Generation wurden als „Gastarbeiter" bezeichnet: Personen, denen aufgrund von Anwerbeabkommen ein zeitlich befristeter Aufenthalt in Ländern wie der BRD, Österreich oder der Schweiz gewährt wurde, um Arbeitskräftemangel auszugleichen. Trotz der Ironie, die in der Verwendung des positiv konnotierten Begriffs „Gast" im Zusammenhang mit der Anwerbung von Arbeitskräften liegt, wurde der Begriff seit den 1970er-Jahren in Österreich als umgangssprachliche Bezeichnung für Arbeitsmigrant*innen verwendet. Studien zeigen, dass es keinen statistischen Zusammenhang zwischen hohen Zuwanderungsraten und hoher → Arbeitslosigkeit gibt. Im

Gegenteil, eine hohe Zuwanderung kann die Wirtschaft ankurbeln und die Arbeitslosigkeit senken, insbesondere bei Geringqualifizierten.

Arbeitskräftemangel
→ Arbeitslos

Arbeitsteilung
→ Kooperation

Arbeitsverdichtung
Fast die Hälfte aller Erwerbstätigen steht täglich unter arbeitsbedingtem Stress. Arbeitsverdichtung beschreibt eine Situation, in der Arbeitnehmer*innen mit einem höheren Arbeitspensum oder zusätzlichen Aufgaben belastet werden. Diese Belastung kann verschiedene Ursachen haben, z. B. Unternehmensziele, technologische Veränderungen, Personalabbau, erhöhte Arbeitsanforderungen oder Umstrukturierungen. Sie ist in vielen modernen Arbeitsumgebungen weit verbreitet und kann sich negativ auf die Gesundheit und das Wohlbefinden der Beschäftigten auswirken und sogar zu → Burnout führen.

Ausbeutung
Menschenhandel und Arbeitsausbeutung sind schwere Menschenrechtsverletzungen, von denen Frauen, Männer und Kinder gleichermaßen betroffen sind – nach Schätzungen der Internationalen Arbeitsorganisation (ILO) rund 40 Millionen Menschen weltweit. Wurden diese hierzulande lange Zeit ausschließlich mit sexueller Ausbeutung in Verbindung gebracht, rückt nun zunehmend der Menschenhandel zum Zweck der Arbeitsausbeutung in den Vordergrund – vor allem im Baugewerbe, in der Landwirtschaft, in der Gastronomie und im Tourismus oder in privaten Haushalten und im Pflegebereich.

Aussperrung
→ Streik

Bullshit-Jobs
Bullshit-Jobs sind Tätigkeiten, die oft selbst von denjenigen, die sie ausüben, als sinnlos empfunden werden. Die Theorie wurde von dem Anthropologen David Graeber geprägt. Bullshit-Jobs sind nicht zu verwechseln mit „Scheiß-Jobs", gesellschaftlich nützlicher Arbeit mit geringem Sozialprestige. Graeber identifizierte fünf Kategorien: „Lakaien", deren Sinn darin besteht, anderen ein Gefühl von Wichtigkeit zu vermitteln; „Schläger", die andere Unternehmen in Schach halten (z. B. PR-Spezialist*innen); „Flickschuster", die nur die Symptome von Problemen temporär lösen; „Kästchenankreuzer", die bloß mit der Dokumentation von Arbeit beschäftigt sind; und „Aufgabenverteiler", die ihre Zeit damit verbringen, sinnlose Aufgaben für andere zu erfinden, z. B. im Management.

Burnout
Überlastung im beruflichen oder privaten Umfeld kann zu einem Syndrom führen – dem Ausbrennen. Burnout wurde erstmals 1974 von dem amerikanischen Psychotherapeuten Herbert J. Freudenberger beschrieben und galt damals als Problem von Menschen in Sozialberufen. Burnout ist keine Krankheit, sondern die Erschöpfung steht im Mittelpunkt einer Reihe von Symptomen wie Schlaflosigkeit, sozialer Rückzug, verminderte Leistungsfähigkeit oder Abstumpfung. Burnout ist ein Risikofaktor für andere Erkrankungen, bei denen Dauerstress eine wichtige Rolle spielt: Depressionen, Angststörungen oder Alkohol- und Medikamentenabhängigkeit. Untersuchungen zufolge erfüllen heute bis zu 1/3 der Erwerbstätigen die Kriterien eines Burnouts oder einer Vorstufe dazu.

Care-Arbeit
→ Sorgearbeit

Clickworker
→ Crowdsourcing

Crowdsourcing
Crowd + Outsourcing. Diese beiden Begriffe zusammen ergeben Crowdsourcing, also die Nutzung der Intelligenz und Arbeitskraft vieler Menschen für Entwicklungs- und Kreativprozesse von Unternehmen. Eines der bekanntesten Beispiele für Crowdsourcing ist Wikipedia, die Online-Enzyklopädie, an der Tausende von Autor*innen beteiligt sind. Viele Unternehmen haben das Potenzial der „Schwarmintelligenz" erkannt. Zum Teil unter Beteiligung finanzieller Anreize, häufig jedoch auch ohne Gegenleistung sind Internetnutzer*innen zur Mitarbeit bereit. Die bezahlte Form des Crowdsourcing wird als Mikrojob bezeichnet. Die Arbeitsleistung wird online erbracht und in der Regel nicht nach Arbeitszeit, sondern nach erledigter Aufgabe bezahlt. Als sogenannte Clickworker trainieren beispielsweise unzählige Menschen in Niedriglohnländern Anwendungen → künstlicher Intelligenz (KI).

Einkommensverteilung
Die Verteilung des in einer Volkswirtschaft in einem Jahr erwirtschafteten Gesamteinkommens kann nach verschiedenen Gesichtspunkten analysiert werden. Zur Berechnung der Einkommens- und Vermögensverteilung wird der Gini-Koeffizient herangezogen, der immer zwischen 0 und 1 liegt. Je höher der Koeffizient, desto ungleicher ist die Verteilung. Im weltweiten Vergleich zählen Norwegen, die Schweiz und Slowenien zu den Ländern mit den niedrigsten Gini-Koeffizienten, während die USA oder Rumänien am oberen Ende der Skala liegen. Bezogen auf das Markteinkommen, also das Einkommen vor staatlicher Umverteilung durch Steuern und Sozialleistungen, hat Österreich einen Gini-Koeffizienten von 0,466, der aber durch Umverteilung halbiert wird (Quelle: WIFO 2023).

Entgrenzung
→ Flexibilität

Erwerbsarmut
Rund 300.000 Personen, 8 % der berufstätigen Bevölkerung in Österreich, sind von Erwerbsarmut betroffen, sogenannte Working Poor. Darunter versteht man Personen, deren monatliches Einkommen trotz Erwerbstätigkeit unter der Armutsgefährdungsschwelle liegt. Als armutsgefährdet gilt, wer mit weniger als 60 % des Medianeinkommens der Gesamtbevölkerung auskommen muss. Derzeit liegt diese Schwelle in Österreich bei rund 1.400 €/Monat für einen Einpersonenhaushalt. Seit 2020 wird ein starker Anstieg an Working Poor verzeichnet, der vor allem auf die Zunahme prekärer Beschäftigungsverhältnisse zurückzuführen ist. Besonders betroffen sind Alleinerzieher*innen und Teilzeitkräfte.

Fair Pay
→ Kulturarbeit

Flexibilität
Autonomie ist der Leitstern unserer Kultur. Wir wollen uns frei entscheiden, tun und lassen, was wir wollen. Diese Maxime wird neuerdings auch in der Arbeitswelt in Form von flexiblen Arbeitszeiten und -orten gefordert. Wahlfreiheit klingt in der Theorie vielversprechend, birgt aber ein Paradox: Flexibilität ist gut, aber sie gibt mir auch die Möglichkeit, Pausen auszulassen und andere Lebensbereiche zugunsten der Arbeit zu vernachlässigen. Beschleunigungs- und Flexibilisierungsmechanismen führen zudem zu einer zunehmenden Entgrenzung zwischen Erwerbsarbeit und privaten Lebensbereichen wie Familie und Haushalt. → New Work

Frauenquote
Die Frauenquote ist eine politische Maßnahme, die darauf abzielt, die Vertretung von Frauen in Führungspositionen zu erhöhen, um → Ungleichheiten zwischen den Geschlechtern zu reduzieren. Sie geht über die bloße Erreichung eines fairen Zahlenverhältnisses zwischen Männern und Frauen hinaus und betrachtet Diversität als ein vielschichtiges Konzept. Derzeit ist die binäre Geschlechterquote oft der kleinste gemeinsame Nenner für Vielfalt in der EU. Der „Thomas-Zyklus" oder „Unconscious Bias" spielt eine entscheidende Rolle bei der Geschlechterungleichheit am Arbeits-

platz. Dieser Kreislauf beschreibt die Tendenz, Personen mit ähnlichem Hintergrund oder Geschlecht zu bevorzugen. Das Hauptargument für die Frauenquote ist der „Trickle-Down-Effekt", der besagt, dass eine Erhöhung des Frauenanteils in Führungspositionen sich auch auf die unteren Ebenen auswirkt. Studien zeigen zwar, dass dies nicht immer der Fall ist. Dennoch können Frauen in Machtpositionen Geschlechterstereotype aufbrechen und das Selbstbild von Frauen positiv beeinflussen.

Freizeit
Bis in die 1980er-Jahre schien die Arbeitszeit ständig abzunehmen. Seither ist jedoch das Gegenteil der Fall. Der → Acht-Stunden-Tag, eine Errungenschaft des 19. Jahrhunderts, entspricht nicht mehr den Anforderungen der Gegenwart, die von permanenter Erreichbarkeit und hohen Leistungsanforderungen geprägt ist. Die Vier-Tage-Woche etwa (also 34 Stunden Arbeit bei vollem Lohn) bietet nicht nur mehr Zeit für dringend benötigte Erholungspausen, sondern eröffnet auch Möglichkeiten für eine Mitgestaltung der Gesellschaft. Die umfangreichste Untersuchung zur Vier-Tage-Woche, 2023 mit 61 britischen Unternehmen und nahezu 3.000 Angestellten durchgeführt, brachte erstaunliche Ergebnisse: Zum Beispiel sank die Anzahl der Krankheitstage um 65 %.

Gastarbeiter
→ Arbeitsmigration

Gewerkschaft
Die Ursprünge der Gewerkschaftsbewegung liegen in der ersten Hälfte des 19. Jahrhunderts. Arbeitervereine waren die Vorläufer der Gewerkschaften und beruhten auf dem Solidaritätsprinzip: Wenn ein*e Arbeiter*in krank wurde oder starb, zahlten diese aus sogenannten Unterstützungskassen Geld an die Familie aus, um sie vor Verarmung zu bewahren. Die erste Gewerkschaft („Vakbond") wurde 1842 von Schriftsetzern in Brüssel gegründet. Belgien hat auch heute noch einen der höchsten gewerkschaftlichen Organisationsgrade in Europa. In Island sind sogar 91 % der Erwerbstätigen gewerkschaftlich organisiert. Der Österreichische Gewerkschaftsbund (ÖGB) zählte Ende 2023 rund 1.200.000 Mitglieder, das sind etwa 27 % der Erwerbstätigen in Österreich.

Globalisierung
Globalisierung beschreibt die zunehmende wirtschaftliche, soziale, kulturelle und politische Verflechtung von Ländern. Befürworter*innen betrachten sie als Motor für wirtschaftliches Wachstum und technologischen Fortschritt, während Kritiker*innen den Welthandel als treibende Kraft für soziale Ungleichheit, Umweltzerstörung und kulturelle Homogenisierung sehen, von dem vor allem multinationale Konzerne profitieren. Denn die Förderung von Freihandel und Deregulierung ermöglicht es globalen Unternehmen, Arbeitsplätze zu verlagern, Löhne zu drücken und Umweltstandards zu umgehen. Dies verstärkt auch die wirtschaftliche Abhängigkeit der Länder des Südens von den Industrieländern des Nordens und verschärft damit strukturelle → Ungleichheiten.

Hausfrau
Der Begriff Hausfrau stammt aus dem 16. Jahrhundert und wurde lange Zeit als Synonym für Ehefrau verwendet. Im traditionellen bürgerlichen Familienmodell des 19. Jahrhunderts wurde zwischen dem „männlichen Ernährer" und dem weiblichen Pendant, der „Hausfrau und Mutter", unterschieden, was angeblich dem „natürlichen Beruf der Frau" entsprach. Dieses Modell blieb bis tief ins 20. Jahrhundert in der Gesellschaft verankert und brach erst langsam durch emanzipatorische Errungenschaften auf. In Österreich dürfen Frauen erst seit 1975 ohne Zustimmung des Ehemannes erwerbstätig sein. Ende der 1990er-Jahre forderte schließlich eine Kampagne der damaligen SPÖ-Frauenministerin Helga Konrad unter dem Motto „Halbe-halbe", dass Frauen und Männer auch in der Hausarbeit gleichberechtigt sein sollten.

Homeoffice
Spätestens seit der Corona-Pandemie arbeiten immer mehr Menschen von zu Hause aus. Dies hat dazu geführt, dass in Österreich seit Frühjahr 2021 neue gesetzliche Rahmen-

bedingungen für das Arbeiten im Homeoffice geschaffen wurden. Das Arbeiten im Homeoffice ist nur auf freiwilliger Basis möglich und muss auf einer Vereinbarung zwischen der Arbeitgeberseite und den Arbeitnehmer*innen beruhen. Homeoffice und → New Work sind eng miteinander verbunden, da beide Konzepte auf → Flexibilität, Selbstbestimmung und eine neue Arbeitskultur abzielen. So ermöglichen Homeoffice und Remote Work, also generell das Arbeiten außerhalb des traditionellen Bürostandortes, den Arbeitnehmer*innen, ihre Aufgaben von zu Hause oder jedem anderen Ort aus zu erledigen, was ein zentrales Element von New Work ist – nämlich die Entgrenzung von Arbeitszeit und Arbeitsort.

KI
Das Thema Künstliche Intelligenz (KI) ist heute allgegenwärtig und zieht viel Aufmerksamkeit auf sich. In der Tat bietet KI in der Arbeitswelt sowohl Chancen als auch Herausforderungen, zumal immer mehr Unternehmen ihre Entscheidungen mithilfe von KI-Systemen treffen. Dies eröffnet zwei extreme Szenarien: Einerseits könnte KI den Weg in eine dystopische Arbeitswirklichkeit ebnen, in der Arbeit entwertet und Menschen zu bloßen Anhängseln von → Maschinen degradiert werden, während Überwachung allgegenwärtig ist. Andererseits könnten KI-gestützte Systeme als Werkzeuge eingesetzt werden, um die Arbeit zu erleichtern und die Arbeitszeit zu verkürzen.

Kooperation
Das Konzept der Arbeitsteilung (Kooperation) geht auf die Aussagen von Adam Smith in *The Wealth of Nations* (1776) zurück. Smith, der als Vordenker der sozialen Marktwirtschaft gilt, stellte fest, dass die Spezialisierung und die Entwicklung von Fähigkeiten in einem bestimmten Bereich die Produktivität der Beteiligten erhöht. Durch diesen Austausch werden mehr und vielfältigere Produkte hergestellt, sodass die*der Einzelne besser versorgt ist.

Kulturarbeit
Interessensvertretungen und → Gewerkschaften der Kulturbranche haben in den letzten Jahren viel Zeit und Energie in die Entwicklung von Richtlinien für eine gerechte Entlohnung künstlerischer und kultureller Arbeit investiert. Denn eine angemessene Entlohnung ist in diesem Bereich alles andere als üblich. Viele Künstler*innen und die Betreiber*innen kleiner Kulturinitiativen leben unter prekären Bedingungen. Da ihre Tätigkeit als → sinnstiftend empfunden wird und Geld nur eine untergeordnete Rolle spielt, neigen Kunst- und Kulturschaffende zur Selbstausbeutung. Weltweite Kampagnen für faire Bedingungen im Kunst- und Kulturbereich haben in den letzten Jahren jedoch einen wichtigen Beitrag geleistet, um das Problembewusstsein zu schärfen und die Branche zu sensibilisieren.

Maschine
Als Ende des 18. Jahrhunderts die ersten Dampfmaschinen in Betrieb genommen wurden, bedeutete dies eine Revolution in der Arbeitswelt. Maschineneinsatz eröffnete neue Effizienz- und Produktionsmöglichkeiten. Gleichzeitig wurden die Arbeiter*innen aus Sicht der Unternehmen mit zunehmender Automatisierung und abnehmendem Bedarf an spezifischem Fachwissen austauschbarer. Die Abhängigkeit von ihren Arbeitgeber*innen wuchs, Arbeitsplatzsicherheit, Qualifikationsanforderungen und die Beziehungen zwischen Arbeitgebenden und Arbeitnehmenden wurden nachhaltig beeinflusst. Maschinen und Automatisierungstechnologien spielen heute eine noch nie dagewesene Rolle in der Arbeitswelt. → KI, Robotik, maschinelles Lernen und hochentwickelte Automatisierungssysteme haben die Arbeitsabläufe in vielen Branchen verändert.

Massengesellschaft
Das Konzept der Massengesellschaft existiert seit der Antike. Der Begriff hat sich über die Zeit verändert und wurde in verschiedenen Regionen unterschiedlich definiert. Heute wird er oft im Kontext der modernen Industriegesellschaften verwendet, in denen die Individualität der*des Einzelnen durch Massenproduktion, Massenmedien und Massenkommunikation beeinflusst wird. In Europa waren sich Kultur- und Kon-

sumkritiker*innen lange Zeit einig, dass Massenproduktion und -vermarktung die Entwicklung autonomer und verantwortungsbewusster Persönlichkeiten stark einschränke. In den USA hingegen bildete sich im 19. Jahrhundert ein Denkmodell heraus, das die Massen- und Konsumgesellschaft positiv bewertete. Es betonte vor allem den individuellen Gewinn durch den Konsum. Im Laufe des 20. Jahrhunderts hat sich das Paradigma des Konsums auch in Europa zu einer kulturellen Dominanz entwickelt.

Menschenhandel
→ Ausbeutung

Mikrojob
→ Crowdsourcing

New Work
New Work ist ein Konzept, das einen neuen Ansatz für die Arbeitswelt beschreibt. Es betont die Idee von → Flexibilität, Selbstbestimmung und → Sinnhaftigkeit der Arbeit. Der Schwerpunkt liegt nicht nur auf der Erledigung von Aufgaben, sondern auch auf der persönlichen Entwicklung, der Selbstverwirklichung und einer guten Work-Life-Balance. New Work fördert agile Organisationsstrukturen, flache Hierarchien, dezentralisierte Entscheidungsfindung und eine Kultur der Zusammenarbeit und Offenheit. Es geht darum, die individuellen Stärken und Potenziale der Mitarbeiter*innen zu erkennen und zu nutzen, um innovative Lösungen zu finden und ein positives Arbeitsumfeld zu schaffen. Insgesamt zielt New Work darauf ab, die Arbeitswelt menschlicher, zukunftsorientierter und anpassungsfähiger zu machen.

Niksen
→ Selbstoptimierung

Null-Stunden-Verträge
Ein Null-Stunden-Vertrag ist eine Sonderform des Arbeits- oder Dienstvertrags. Die Besonderheit liegt daran, dass die*der Arbeitnehmer*in nur bei Bedarf tätig wird und dementsprechend auch nur dann eine Bezahlung erhält. Besonders im Vereinigten Königreich und in den Niederlanden sind diese Verträge stark verbreitet. In beiden Ländern arbeiten je rund eine Million Menschen als Bereitschaftsarbeiter*innen ohne feste Arbeitszeiten.

Pension
Der Ruhestand ist ein beträchtlicher Teil des Lebens. Das gesetzliche Pensionsantrittsalter liegt in Österreich derzeit bei 65 Jahren für Männer und 60 Jahren für Frauen, während die durchschnittliche Lebenserwartung bei 78 Jahren für Männer und 83 Jahren für Frauen liegt. Der demografische Wandel, bei dem einer alternden Gesellschaft künftig weniger Erwerbstätige gegenüberstehen, die die Pensionen für immer mehr Rentner*innen finanzieren müssen, stellt eine finanzielle Herausforderung für die Pensionssysteme dar.

Pensionslücke
Wer im Alter auf eine Mindestpension angewiesen ist, ist in der Regel von Altersarmut betroffen. Das Risiko ist für Frauen deutlich höher als für Männer. Mehr als 2/3 der Armutsbetroffenen in der Altersgruppe der über 65-Jährigen in Österreich sind Frauen. Während die durchschnittliche Bruttopension 2022 bei Männern 2.229 € betrug, lag sie bei Frauen mit 1.313 € um 41,1 % darunter (Quelle: Statistik Austria). Gründe dafür sind unterbrochene Erwerbsbiografien, lange Teilzeitphasen und jahrelange unbezahlte Betreuungsarbeit. Um die Pensionslücke zu schließen, werden zunehmend Forderungen nach einer besseren Anrechnung von Kinderbetreuungs- und Erziehungszeiten sowie Elternteilzeit laut.

Prekär
→ Erwerbsarmut

Produktivität
Arbeitsproduktivität lässt sich als das Verhältnis von Ergebnis zu Arbeitsaufwand definieren. Diese Formel ermöglicht es, die durchschnittliche Arbeitsleistung von Mitarbeiter*innen in einem bestimmten Zeitraum zu berechnen. Sie wird vielfach von Unternehmen genutzt, in denen die Arbeitsergebnisse in Stückzahlen oder Geldeinheiten gemessen werden können, wie beispielsweise in der Logistik, der Landwirtschaft oder der Massenproduktion. Die Arbeitsproduktivität wird häufig als Kennzahl in Bereichen mit gering qualifizierten Tätigkeiten oder Akkordarbeit verwendet. Sie ermöglicht es, Mitarbeiter*innen miteinander zu vergleichen und die Effizienz ihrer Arbeit zu bewerten. Einige Arbeitgeber*innen benutzen die Produktivitätsmessung, um Druck auf die Beschäftigten auszuüben und sie als Grundlage für Entlassungen zu verwenden.

Prokrastinieren
Arbeit aufzuschieben, anstatt sie zu erledigen, kann problematisch und sogar krankhaft werden. Unangenehme Dinge zu vermeiden, kann sich kurzfristig gut anfühlen, obwohl die negativen Auswirkungen des Aufschiebens bekannt sind. Eine Studie zeigt, dass zwei Bevölkerungsgruppen besonders anfällig für Prokrastination sind: Männer unter 30 Jahren und Arbeitslose. Die Gründe dafür liegen in einem Mangel an Struktur bzw. in dem Gefühl, über unbegrenzte Lebenszeit zu verfügen. Eine intensive Mediennutzung ist in diesem Zusammenhang ein zusätzlicher Faktor. Manchmal kann Prokrastination aber nicht nur destruktiv, sondern auch strategisch eingesetzt werden und sich als produktiv erweisen – zum Beispiel, wenn man auf eine ärgerliche E-Mail nicht sofort antwortet.

Quiet Quitting
Früher nannte man es „Dienst nach Vorschrift", heute heißt es „Quiet Quitting": Immer mehr Menschen greifen zu diesem Bewältigungsmechanismus, sei es, weil sie am Arbeitsplatz nicht genug Wertschätzung erfahren, weil sie sich von der Arbeitsbelastung überfordert fühlen oder weil sie ihr Verhältnis zur Arbeit insgesamt infrage stellen. Quiet Quitting bedeutet nicht, innerlich zu kündigen, sondern eine klare Grenze zu ziehen.

Remote Work
→ Homeoffice

Rente
→ Pension

Repetitive Arbeitsabläufe
→ Routine

Routine
Repetitive Arbeitsabläufe gehören für viele Menschen zum Arbeitsalltag. Spricht man von Routine in der Arbeit, so ist dies oft negativ besetzt und wird mit Langeweile und mangelnder Kreativität gleichgesetzt. Automatismen, wie wir sie beispielsweise von Fließbandtätigkeiten kennen, haben den Vorteil, dass Handgriffe schnell, sicher und effizient ausgeführt werden können. Routine ist Teil des sogenannten Gewohnheitskreislaufs und prägt sich ein, verknüpft also bestimmte Situationen mit Verhaltensmustern.

Scheiß-Jobs
→ Bullshit-Jobs

Selbstoptimierung
Die ständige Verfügbarkeit und Aktivität in der kapitalistischen Gesellschaft führen dazu, dass Menschen sich selbst optimieren müssen, um in einer zunehmend wettbewerbsorientierten Arbeitswelt bestehen zu können. Um dem Leistungsdruck und den hohen Anforderungen, die an die Arbeitnehmer*innen gestellt werden, standzuhalten, wird Selbstoptimierung oft als notwendiges Mittel zum Erfolg betrachtet. Ein übermäßiges Streben nach Selbstoptimierung kann jedoch auch zu Stress, → Burnout und anderen Gesundheitsproblemen führen. Da Leistung, Effizienz und → Produktivität einen Ausgleich zum stressigen

Alltag erfordern, für den zunehmend die Zeit fehlt, werden Techniken zum Stressabbau wie Yoga oder Meditation, die „schnelle" Entspannung bringen, immer beliebter. Auch die Umkehrung der Selbstoptimierung, das zweckfreie Faulenzen, ist inzwischen zum Wellnesstrend avanciert: „niksen" ist niederländisch und bedeutet nichts tun.

Sinn
Die Selbstbestimmungstheorie von Richard L. Ryan und Edward L. Deci besagt, dass die Erfüllung der grundlegenden menschlichen Bedürfnisse nach Eingebundenheit, Autonomie und Kompetenz die Motivation fördert. Im Arbeitskontext bedeutet das, dass Tätigkeiten, die diese Bedürfnisse erfüllen, das Wohlbefinden und die Gesundheit fördern. Ein wichtiger Aspekt ist dabei die Sinnhaftigkeit: Arbeit ist dann gesund, wenn sie Sinn und Zweck erfüllt. Sinn ist dabei individuell zu verstehen und bedeutet nicht, dass man einen Beruf ausüben muss, der die Welt verändert. Die Einstellung zur Arbeit ist aber auch eine Generationenfrage und basiert auf unterschiedlichen Wertesystemen. Während Arbeit für die Babyboomer deutlich identitätsstiftender war, hat sie für die Generation Z, also die zwischen 1997 und 2012 Geborenen, eine geringere Priorität als andere Lebensbereiche. Das bedeutet nicht, dass junge Menschen weniger belastbar sind – sie *lassen* sich nur weniger belasten.

Sorgearbeit
Der Zusammenhang zwischen Sorgearbeit und Geschlecht ist historisch nicht zu trennen. Die Pflichten für Kinderbetreuung, Altenpflege und Haushalt werden traditionell Frauen zugeschrieben. Die Hausarbeitsdebatte der 1970er-Jahre führte in der Frauenbewegung zur Forderung nach „Lohn für Hausarbeit". Bis heute wird diskutiert, welche gesellschaftliche Bedeutung die unbezahlte Care-Arbeit hat und warum sie in den letzten Jahrzehnten symbolisch weiter abgewertet wurde.

Stechuhr
→ Stempeluhr

Stempeluhr
Die Stechuhr oder Stempeluhr ist ein Gerät zur Erfassung der Arbeitszeit. Sie wurde Ende des 19. Jahrhunderts entwickelt, um die Anwesenheit von Arbeiter*innen in Fabriken und Büros genau zu erfassen. Die Stechuhr revolutionierte die Arbeitszeiterfassung und trug zur Entstehung standardisierter Arbeitszeiten bei. Sie wurde zum Symbol für Kontrolle und Überwachung am Arbeitsplatz, aber auch für Effizienz und Rationalisierung der Arbeit. Im Laufe der Zeit wurden die Stempeluhren durch elektronische und digitale Systeme ersetzt, die genauere und vielseitigere Methoden der Zeiterfassung ermöglichen. Heute werden auch digitale Kontrollprogramme wie Time Doctor und Terramind verwendet, die beispielsweise die Anzahl der Tastenanschläge zählen.

Streik
Der Streik ist ein mächtiges Mittel im Arbeitskampf, das es Arbeitnehmer*innen ermöglicht, ihre Forderungen durchzusetzen. Die älteste dokumentierte Arbeitsniederlegung fand 1159 vor der Zeitenwende im alten Ägypten beim Bau der Königsgräber in Theben statt. Der Begriff „Streik" leitet sich vom englischen Wort „strike" ab, das auf eine nautische Redewendung zurückgeht. Im Jahr 1768 legten Seeleute in Sunderland die Arbeit nieder, indem sie die Segel einholten, was als „strike sails" bezeichnet wird. In Österreich sind Streiks und kollektive Arbeitsniederlegungen grundrechtlich geschützt. Arbeitnehmer*innen haben das Recht, → Gewerkschaften zu bilden und sich an Streiks zu beteiligen, ohne Folgen wie Kündigung oder Schadenersatzansprüche fürchten zu müssen. Das Gegenstück zum Streik ist die Aussperrung, bei der Arbeitnehmer*innen an der Aufnahme ihrer Arbeit gehindert werden, üblicherweise als Druckmittel der Arbeitgeber*innen im Zuge eines Arbeitskampfes.

Stress
→ Burnout

Überwachung
→ Stempeluhr

Ungleichheit
Die globale Corona-Pandemie von 2020/21 hat alle getroffen, aber nicht alle in gleichem Maße. Die Krise hat viele soziale Ungleichheiten nicht nur aufgedeckt, sondern auch verstärkt. Österreich gilt im internationalen Vergleich oft als Land des sozialen Ausgleichs, doch dieser Ruf beruht auf einem starken Sozialstaat und entspricht nicht mehr der Realität. Tatsächlich zählt Österreich zu den Ländern mit den größten Vermögens- und Einkommensunterschieden. → Globalisierung → Einkommensverteilung

Unsichtbare Arbeit
Nicht alle Leistungen sind messbar, geschweige denn bezahlt. Gerade Frauen erledigen viele Tätigkeiten im Haushalt und für die Familie ganz selbstverständlich und stillschweigend – oft neben ihrem Teilzeit- oder Vollzeitjob. Das traditionelle Rollenbild und die hohen Anforderungen, die die Gesellschaft an Frauen stellt, werden meist nicht hinterfragt. Unsichtbare Leistungen können zur psychischen Belastung werden – zum Mental Load. Damit ist die Belastung durch ständige Planungs- und Koordinationsaufgaben gemeint, die der Alltag mit sich bringt. → Sorgearbeit

Vier-Tage-Woche
→ Freizeit

Wanderarbeiter*innen
→ Arbeitsmigration

Welthandel
→ Globalisierung

Wertschätzung
→ Quiet Quitting

Wertschöpfungskette
Die Wertschöpfungskette, auch Wertkette genannt, beschreibt die Prozesse, die Unternehmen durchführen, um ein Produkt herzustellen und einen Mehrwert zu schaffen. Die Idee der Wertschöpfungskette geht auf den amerikanischen Wirtschaftswissenschaftler Michael E. Porter zurück. In der heutigen globalisierten Wirtschaft ist die Wertschöpfung für Unternehmen ein entscheidender Faktor, um sich von der Konkurrenz abzuheben und langfristig erfolgreich zu sein. Die Bewertung sozialer Aspekte entlang der Wertschöpfungskette wie faire Entlohnung, Gesundheitsschutz oder Arbeitssicherheit wird im Gegensatz zur ökonomischen Betrachtung jedoch noch wenig berücksichtigt.

Working Poor
→ Erwerbsarmut

Zeit
Die Zeitökonomie beschäftigt sich mit der Bewertung und Nutzung der Ressource Zeit in wirtschaftlichen und gesellschaftlichen Zusammenhängen. Trotz wachsender Bestrebungen nach Autonomie und → Flexibilität fehlt vielen Menschen die Kontrolle über ihre Zeit. Die Notwendigkeit, Zeit an Arbeitgeber*innen zu verkaufen, wird durch Lohnverhältnisse beeinflusst und widerspiegelt Muster von Ermächtigung und Entmündigung. Benjamin Franklins berühmter Ausspruch „Zeit ist Geld" verdeutlicht die Reduzierung von Zeit auf eine handelbare Ware. Doch die Frage, wer den Wert der Zeit bestimmt und nach welchem Zeitplan sich andere richten sollen, bleibt in dieser Diskussion zentral.

Zeiterfassung
→ Stempeluhr

Glossary

24/7
24 hours a day, 7 days a week – in other words, around the clock. This abbreviation, originally introduced in the USA in the 1980s, has become increasingly widespread with the development of modern means of communication and the associated constant availability of goods and services. Today, 24/7 is also associated with constant reachability, e.g. in the context of customer service – a marketing buzzword that suggests always being available. Hence 24/7 also stands for shift operation.

AI
The topic of artificial intelligence (AI) is everywhere these days and attracts a lot of attention. In fact, AI offers both opportunities and challenges in the world of work, especially as a growing number of companies are making their decisions with the help of AI systems. This opens up two extreme scenarios: on the one hand, AI could pave the way to a dystopian working reality in which labour is devalued and humans are degraded to mere appendages of machines, while surveillance is omnipresent. On the other hand, AI-supported systems could be used as tools to make work easier and reduce working hours.

appreciation
→ quiet quitting

bullshit jobs
Bullshit jobs are professions that are perceived as pointless, often even by those doing them. The term was proposed by anthropologist David Graeber. Bullshit jobs are not to be confused with shit jobs, which are socially useful jobs with low social prestige. Graeber identified five categories of bullshit jobs: 'flunkies' whose purpose is to make others feel important; 'goons' who keep other companies in check (e.g. PR specialists); 'duct tapers' who only temporarily solve the symptoms of problems; 'box tickers' who are only concerned with documenting work; and 'taskmasters' who spend their time inventing meaningless tasks for others, e.g. in management.

burnout
Overwork in the professional or private environment can lead to a syndrome – burnout. The term burnout was first described in 1974 by the American psychotherapist Herbert J. Freudenberger and at that time was considered a problem for people in social professions. Burnout is not an illness in the narrower sense, but exhaustion is at the centre of a series of symptoms such as insomnia, social withdrawal, reduced performance or dullness. Burnout is a risk factor for other illnesses in which permanent stress plays an important role: depression, anxiety disorders or alcohol and drug addiction. According to various studies, up to 1/3 of people in employment today fulfil the criteria for burnout or a preliminary stage of burnout.

care work
The connection between care work and gender is historically inextricable. Childcare, elderly care and household chores are traditionally assigned to women. The housework debate of the 1970s led to the demand for 'wages for housework' in the women's movement. To this day, there is debate about the social significance of unpaid care work and why it has been symbolically devalued in recent decades.

clickworker
→ crowdsourcing

cooperation
The concept of the division of labour (cooperation) goes back to the statements made by Adam Smith in *The Wealth of Nations* (1776). Smith, who is regarded as the mastermind of the social market economy, observed that specialisation and the development

of skills in a particular area increases the productivity of those involved. Through this exchange, more and increasingly diverse products are made, so that the individual is better provided for.

crowdsourcing
Crowd + outsourcing. These two terms together make up crowdsourcing, i.e. the use of the intelligence and labour of many people for the development and creative processes of companies. One of the best-known examples of crowdsourcing is Wikipedia, the online encyclopaedia in which thousands of authors are involved. Many companies have recognised the potential of 'swarm intelligence'. Internet users are willing to collaborate, sometimes with financial incentives, but often for nothing in return. The paid form of crowdsourcing is known as a microjob. The work is performed online and is usually not paid by the hour, but by the task completed. For example, countless people in low-wage countries train → artificial intelligence (AI) applications as so-called clickworkers.

cultural work
In recent years, interest groups and → trade unions in the cultural sector have invested a great deal of time and energy into developing guidelines for fair pay for artistic and cultural work. After all, fair pay is anything but common in this sector. Many artists and operators of small cultural initiatives live in precarious conditions. As their work is perceived as → meaningful and money only plays a subordinate role, artists and cultural workers tend to exploit themselves. However, global campaigns for fair conditions in the arts and culture sector have made an important contribution in recent years to raising awareness of the problem and sensitising the industry.

division of labour
→ cooperation

eight-hour day
With the slogan '8 hours labour, 8 hours recreation, 8 hours rest', the Welsh entrepreneur and social reformer Robert Owen launched the campaign to reduce working hours and improve working conditions. This was led by the → trade union movement in Great Britain, which had been gaining strength since the 1830s. In Austria, the eight-hour working day was introduced after the end of the First World War. From January 1919, it applied to all employees in private and public companies – with exceptions such as agriculture.

exploitation
Human trafficking and labour exploitation are serious human rights violations that affect women, men and children equally – around 40 million people worldwide, according to estimates by the International Labour Organization (ILO). While this was long associated exclusively with sexual exploitation in this country, human trafficking for the purpose of labour exploitation is now increasingly coming to the fore – especially in the construction industry, agriculture, gastronomy and tourism or in private households and the care sector.

fair pay
→ cultural work

flexibility
Autonomy is the guiding star of our culture. We want to be free to decide, do and leave whatever we want. Recently, this maxim has also been demanded in the world of work in the form of flexible working hours and locations (→ New Work). Freedom of choice sounds promising in theory, but it harbours a paradox: flexibility is good, but it also gives me the opportunity to skip breaks and neglect other areas of life in favour of work. Acceleration and flexibilisation mechanisms also lead to an increasing imbalance and blurring of boundaries between gainful employment and private areas of life such as family and household.

four-day week
→ free time

free time
Until the 1980s, it seemed that working hours would steadily decrease. Since then, however, the opposite has been the case. The → eight-hour day, an achievement of the 19th century, no longer meets the demands of the present, which is characterised by permanent availability and high performance requirements. The four-day week, for example (i.e. 34 hours of work with full pay), not only offers more time for much-needed relaxation breaks, but also opens up opportunities for active participation in shaping society. The most comprehensive study on the four-day week, conducted with 61 British companies and almost 3,000 employees in 2023, produced remarkable results: For example, the number of sick days fell by 65%.

global trade
→ globalisation

globalisation
Globalisation describes the increasing economic, social, cultural and political interdependence of countries. Proponents see it as an engine for economic growth and technological progress, while critics see global trade as a driving force behind social inequality, environmental destruction and cultural homogenisation, which primarily benefits multinational corporations and financial institutions. This is because the promotion of free trade and deregulation enables global companies to relocate jobs, depress wages and circumvent environmental standards. This also increases the economic dependence of the countries of the South on the industrialised countries of the North and thus exacerbates structural → inequalities.

guest workers
→ labour migration

home office
Ever since the coronavirus pandemic, a growing number of people have been working from home. As a result, new legal framework conditions for working from home have been in place in Austria since spring 2021. Working from home is only possible on a voluntary basis and must be based on an agreement between the employer and the employee. Working from home and New Work are closely linked, as both concepts are aimed at → flexibility, self-determination and a new work culture. Home office and remote work, i.e. working outside the traditional office location in general, enable employees to carry out their tasks from home or any other location, which is a central element of → New Work – namely the dissolution of boundaries between working hours and place of work.

housewife
The term 'housewife' dates back to the 16th century and was long used as a synonym for 'wife'. In the traditional bourgeois family model of the 19th century, a distinction was made between the 'male breadwinner' and the female counterpart, the 'housewife and mother', which supposedly corresponded to a woman's 'natural profession'. This model remained anchored in society well into the 20th century and was only slowly broken down by emancipatory achievements. In Austria, women have only been allowed to work without their husbands' consent since 1975. At the end of the 1990s, a campaign by the then SPÖ Women's Minister Helga Konrad under the motto 'Halbe-halbe' (half and half) finally demanded that women and men should also have equal duties in housework.

human trafficking
→ exploitation

imbalance
→ flexibility

income distribution
The distribution of the total income generated in an economy in one year can be analysed according to various aspects. The Gini coefficient, which is always between 0 and 1, is used to calculate the distribution of income and wealth. The higher the coefficient, the more unequal the distribution. In a global comparison, Norway, Switzerland and Slovenia are among the countries with the lowest Gini coefficients, while the USA and Romania are at the upper end of the scale. In terms of market income, i.e. income before state redistribution through taxes and social benefits, Austria has a Gini coefficient of 0.466, which is actually halved through redistribution (source: WIFO 2023).

inequality
The global coronavirus pandemic of 2020/21 has affected everyone, but not to the same extent. The crisis has not only exposed many social inequalities, but also exacerbated them. By international standards, Austria is often regarded as a country of social equalisation, but this reputation is based on a strong welfare state and no longer corresponds to reality. In fact, Austria is one of the countries with the greatest wealth and income disparities. → globalisation → income distribution

invisible work
Not all work can be measured, nor is it paid. Women in particular do many household and family tasks quite naturally and silently – often in addition to their part-time or full-time job. The traditional gender roles and the high demands that society places on women usually remain unquestioned. Invisible achievements can become a psychological burden – a mental load. This refers to the burden of constant planning and coordination tasks that everyday life entails.

in-work poverty
Around 300,000 people, or 8% of the working population in Austria, are affected by in-work poverty, the so-called working poor. This refers to people whose monthly income is below the at-risk-of-poverty threshold despite being employed. People are considered to be at risk of poverty if they have to live on less than 60% of the median income of the overall population – this threshold in Austria is currently around € 1,400 per month for a single-person household. Since 2020, there has been a sharp rise in the number of working poor, which is mainly due to the increase in precarious employment. Single parents and part-time workers are also particularly affected.

itinerant workers
→ labour migration

labour dispute
→ strike

labour migration
Labour migration, also known as employment migration, refers to migration primarily for the purpose of taking up or changing gainful employment. The term 'guest worker' refers to people who were granted temporary residence in countries such as the Federal Republic of Germany, Austria or Switzerland to take up gainful employment on the basis of labour recruitment agreements. After the Second World War in particular, many European countries recruited 'guest workers', especially from southern Europe. Despite the irony of using the positively connoted word 'guest' in connection with a framework agreement for the recruitment of labour, the expression has been used as a colloquial term for migrant workers in Austria since the 1970s. Studies show that there is no statistical correlation between high immigration rates and high unemployment. On the contrary, high immigration can boost the economy and reduce → unemployment, especially among low-skilled workers.

labour movement
During the period of industrialisation at the beginning of the 19th century, a new impoverished underclass emerged – the 'working class'. Poverty and misery often erupted into unrest. Soon solidarity organisations were formed. From the 1830s, there were organised protests for better working conditions, fairer wages and the recognition of trade unions. During the revolution of 1848, which had a major influence on the labour movement, important foundations were laid for the reduction of working hours (10-hour day) and wage increases.

labour shortage
→ unemployed

lockout
→ strike

machine
When the first steam engines were put into operation at the end of the 18th century, it signalled a revolution in the world of work. The use of machines opened up new opportunities for efficiency and production. At the same time, as automation increased and the need for specific expertise decreased, workers became more interchangeable from an employer's perspective. Their dependence on their employers grew, job security, qualification requirements and relations between employers and employees were permanently affected. Machines and automation technologies now play an unprecedented role in the world of work. → Artificial intelligence, robotics, machine learning and sophisticated automation systems have changed work processes in many industries.

mass society
The concept of mass society has existed since ancient times. The term has changed over time and has been defined differently in different regions. Today, it is often used in the context of modern industrialised societies, in which the individuality of the individual is influenced by mass production, mass media and mass communication. In Europe, cultural and consumer critics long agreed that mass production and mass marketing severely restricted the development of autonomous and responsible personalities. In the USA, on the other hand, a model of thought emerged in the 19th century that took a positive view of mass and consumer society. Above all, it emphasised individual gain through consumption. Over the course of the 20th century, the paradigm of consumption also assumed cultural dominance in Europe.

meaning
The self-determination theory of Richard L. Ryan and Edward L. Deci states that the fulfilment of the basic human needs for involvement, autonomy and competence promotes motivation. In the work context, this means that the activities that fulfil these needs promote well-being and health. An important aspect here is meaningfulness: work is healthy when it fulfils meaning and purpose. Meaning is to be understood individually and does not imply that you have to do a job that changes the world. However, attitudes towards work are also a generational issue and are based on different value systems. While work was clearly more identity-forming for baby boomers, it has a lower priority than other areas of life for Generation Z, i.e. those born between 1997 and 2012. This does not mean that young people are unable to work under pressure – they are just less willing to be put under pressure.

microjob
→ crowdsourcing

New Work
New Work is a concept describing a new approach to the world of work that differs from traditional models. It emphasises the idea of → flexibility, self-determination and → meaningfulness of work. The focus is not only on completing tasks, but also on

personal development, self-realisation and a good work-life balance. New Work promotes agile organisational structures, flat hierarchies, decentralised decision-making and a culture of collaboration and openness. It is about recognising and utilising the individual strengths and potential of employees in order to find innovative solutions and create a positive working environment. Overall, New Work aims to make the world of work more human, future-oriented and adaptable.

niksen
→ self-optimisation

pension gap
Those who are dependent on a minimum pension in later life are generally affected by old-age poverty. The risk is significantly higher for women than for men: more than 2/3 of those affected by poverty in the over-65 age group in Austria are women. While in 2022 the average gross pension for men was € 2,229, it was 41.1% lower for women at € 1,313 (source: Statistics Austria). The reasons for this are interrupted employment histories, long periods of part-time work and years of unpaid care work. In order to close the pension gap, there are increasing calls for better recognition of childcare periods, parental part-time work and parental leave.

precarious
→ in-work poverty

procrastinating
Putting off work instead of getting it done can become problematic and even pathological. Avoiding unpleasant things can feel good in the short term, although the negative effects of procrastination are well known. One study shows two population groups as being particularly prone to procrastination: men under the age of 30 and the unemployed. The reasons for this lie in a lack of structure or the feeling that they have unlimited time at their disposal. Intensive media use is an additional factor in this context. Sometimes, however, procrastination is not just destructive but can be used strategically and prove productive – for example, not replying immediately to an annoying email.

productivity
Labour productivity can be defined as the ratio of output to labour input. This formula makes it possible to calculate the average labour output of employees over a certain period of time. It is often used by companies in which the results of labour can be measured in quantities or monetary units, such as in logistics, agriculture or mass production. Labour productivity is often used as a key figure in areas with low-skilled activities or piecework. It allows comparison between employees and an assessment of the efficiency of their work. Some employers use productivity measurement to put pressure on employees and as a basis for dismissals.

punch clock
→ time clock

quiet quitting
It used to be called 'working to rule', today it is known as 'quiet quitting': a growing number of people are resorting to this coping mechanism, whether it is because they do not feel sufficiently valued at work, because they are overwhelmed by the workload or because they are questioning their relationship to work as a whole. Quiet quitting does not mean quitting internally – rather, it is about drawing a clear boundary.

remote work
→ home office

repetitive work processes
→ routine

retirement
Retirement is a substantial part of life. The statutory retirement age in Austria is currently 65 years for men and 60 years for women, while the average life expectancy is 78 years for men and 83 years for women. Demographic change poses a financial challenge for pension systems: an ageing society will in future be faced with fewer people in employment having to finance the pensions of a growing number of pensioners.

routine
For many people, repetitive work processes are part of their everyday working life. When we talk about routine at work it often has negative connotations and is equated with boredom and a lack of creativity. Automated processes, such as assembly line activities, have the advantage that tasks can be carried out quickly, safely and efficiently. Routines are part of the so-called cycle of habits and become ingrained, linking certain situations with behavioural patterns.

self-optimisation
Constant availability and activity in a capitalist society mean that people have to optimise themselves in order to survive in an increasingly competitive working world. In order to endure the pressure to perform and the high demands placed on employees, self-optimisation is often seen as a necessary means to success. However, excessive striving for self-optimisation can also lead to stress, → burnout and other health problems. As performance, efficiency and → productivity require a balance to stressful everyday life, for which there is increasingly no time, stress reduction techniques such as yoga or meditation, which provide 'quick' relaxation, are becoming increasingly popular. The reversal of self-optimisation, lazing around without purpose, has also become a wellness trend: 'niksen' is the Dutch concept of 'doing nothing'.

shit jobs
→ bullshit jobs

stress
→ burnout

strike
Strikes are a powerful tool in labour disputes, allowing workers to push through their collective demands. The oldest documented work stoppage took place in 1159 BCE in ancient Egypt during the construction of the royal tombs at Thebes. The word 'strike' can be traced back to a nautical expression: in 1768, sailors in Sunderland stopped work by taking down their sails, or 'striking sails'. In Austria, strikes and collective work stoppages are constitutionally protected. Employees have the right to form → trade unions and take part in strikes without having to fear consequences such as dismissal or claims for damages. The counterpart to strikes is lockouts, in which employees are prevented from starting work, usually as a means of pressure by the employer in the course of a labour dispute.

surveillance
→ time clock

time
Time economics deals with the evaluation and utilisation of time as a resource in economic and social contexts. Despite growing aspirations for autonomy and → flexibility, many people lack control over their time. The need to sell time to employers is influenced by wage relations and reflects patterns of empowerment and disempowerment. Benjamin Franklin's famous saying 'time is money' illustrates the reduction of time to a tradable commodity. However, the question of who determines the value of time and what schedule others should follow remains central to this discussion.

time clock
The time clock, also known as a punch clock, is a device for recording working hours. It was developed at the end of the 19th century to accurately record the attendance of workers in factories and offices. The time clock revolutionised the recording of working hours and contributed to the emergence of standardised working hours. It became a symbol of control and monitoring in the workplace, but also of efficiency and rationalisation of work. Over time, punch clocks have been replaced by electronic and digital systems that enable more accurate and versatile methods of time recording. Also in use today are digital control programs such as Time Doctor and Terramind, which count the number of keystrokes, for example.

time recording
→ time clock

trade union
The origins of the trade union movement date back to the first half of the 19th century. Workers' associations were the forerunners of trade unions and were based on the principle of solidarity: if a worker fell ill or died, they paid out money to the family from so-called benevolent funds to prevent them from falling into poverty. The first trade union ('Vakbond') was founded by typesetters in Brussels in 1842. Belgium still has one of the highest levels of unionisation in Europe today. In Iceland, 91% of the workforce is unionised. The Austrian Trade Union Federation (ÖGB) had around 1,200,000 members at the end of 2023, which is around 27% of the labour force in Austria.

unemployed
Despite the economic crisis, Austria has comparatively low unemployment rates (as of March 2024: 291,468 people, source: AMS), with many sectors reporting a shortage of labour. Nevertheless, a debate has broken out between the political parties about possible cuts to unemployment benefits or the introduction of a degressive model like in Denmark or Sweden. Currently, the net replacement rate for the unemployed is 55% of the last monthly salary for 20 to 52 weeks, after which it is 51% social assistance. This means that Austria already has one of the lowest net replacement rates in Europe. People with a low level of education and a migrant background are more affected by unemployment, while youth unemployment is also on the rise and the long-term unemployment rate has almost doubled compared to ten years ago.

value chain
The value chain describes the processes that companies carry out to produce a product and create added value. The idea of the value chain originated with the American economist Michael E. Porter. In today's globalised economy, value creation is a crucial factor for companies to differentiate themselves from the competition and to be successful in the long term. However, the assessment of social aspects along the value chain, such as fair pay, health and safety at work, still receives little attention in contrast to the economic viewpoint.

women's quota
The women's quota is a political measure that aims to increase the representation of women in management positions in order to reduce gender → inequality. It goes beyond simply achieving a fair numerical ratio between men and women and views diversity as a multi-layered concept. Currently, the binary gender quota is often the lowest common denominator for diversity in the EU. The 'Thomas Cycle' or 'Unconscious Bias' plays a crucial role in gender inequality in the workplace. This cycle describes the tendency to favour people with a similar background or gender. The main argument in favour of the women's quota is the 'trickle-down effect', which states that an increase in the proportion of women in management positions also has an impact on the lower levels. Studies show that this is not always the case. Nevertheless, women in positions of power can break down gender stereotypes and have a positive influence on women's self-image.

work intensification
Almost half of all employees experience work-related stress on a daily basis. Work intensification describes a situation in which employees are burdened with a higher workload or additional tasks. This stress can have various causes, e.g. company goals, technological changes, downsizing, increased work demands or reorganisation. It is widespread in many modern working environments and can have a negative impact on the health and well-being of employees and can even lead to → burnout.

working class
→ labour movement

working poor
→ in-work poverty

zero-hours contracts
A zero-hours contract is a special form of employment or service contract. It is characterised by the fact that the employee only works when required and therefore only receives payment then. These contracts are particularly widespread in the United Kingdom and the Netherlands. In both countries, around one million people work as on-call workers without fixed working hours.

Biografien

Maja Bajević (1967 Sarajevo/BA) lebt in Paris. Nach Abschluss ihrer klassischen Ausbildung im ehemaligen Jugoslawien studierte sie an der École Nationale Supérieure des Beaux-Arts in Paris. 2017 wurde sie für den Prix Marcel Duchamp vorgeschlagen. Sie nahm an zahlreichen Gruppen- und Einzelausstellungen teil, inklusive der 56. Biennale in Venedig (2015) und der documenta 12 in Kassel (2007). Ihre Werke wurden auch in Ljubljana, Zürich, New York, Madrid, Berlin und München ausgestellt.

Julien Berthier (1975 Besançon/FR) lebt in Paris. Er besuchte die École Nationale Supérieure des Beaux-Arts in Paris und ist seit den frühen 2000ern international tätig. Mit einer Bandbreite von Arbeiten, die Video, Fotografie, Skulptur, Zeichnung und Installationen beinhalten, entzieht er sich strenger Kategorisierung und schafft ungewöhnliche, aber funktionale Werke, die unsere Perspektiven herausfordern. Er nahm an zahlreichen Gruppen- und Einzelausstellungen in Frankreich und im Ausland teil, unter anderem in Wien, Graz, Köln, Brüssel, Peking und Los Angeles.

Louisa Clement (1987 Bonn/DE) lebt in Bonn. Sie studierte an der Staatlichen Akademie der Bildenden Künste Karlsruhe und der Kunstakademie Düsseldorf als Meisterschülerin von Andreas Gursky. Die Künstlerin hat in Institutionen und Museen im In- und Ausland ausgestellt. Ihre Werke sind Teil von Sammlungen wie dem Huis Marseille in Amsterdam, der Atlanta Cultural Foundation in Bad Homburg, der Sammlung der Stadt Brühl und der Ringier Collection in Zürich.

Manuel Correa (1991 Medellín/CO) ist Künstler und Filmemacher. Er studierte Film und Medien an der Emily Carr University in Vancouver und schloss seinen MA in Architektur-Forschung am Goldsmiths College der University of London ab. Seine Arbeiten wurden unter anderem auf dem Internationalen Filmfestival Rotterdam, im Museo Tamayo in Mexiko, auf der 8. Norwegischen Skulpturenbiennale, im Kunsternes Hus in Oslo und im Het Nieuwe Instituut gezeigt. Derzeit arbeitet er als Teil der Gruppe Forensic Architecture.

Jeremy Deller (1966 London/UK) lebt in London. Er studierte Kunstgeschichte am Courtauld Institute und an der University of Sussex. Der Künstler, Kurator und Kulturaktivist ist bekannt für seine sozial engagierten und politisch aufgeladenen Werke. 2004 wurde Deller mit dem renommierten Turner-Preis ausgezeichnet und vertrat Großbritannien 2013 auf der 55. Biennale von Venedig. Er hat weltweit umfangreich ausgestellt, darunter in Buenos Aires, Hongkong, New York, Madrid, Paris und Tokio.

Antje Ehmann (1968 Gelsenkirchen/DE) ist Kuratorin, Autorin und Künstlerin mit Sitz in Berlin. Sie arbeitete viele Jahre mit ihrem Lebensgefährten Harun Farocki zusammen und ist derzeit als Verwalterin seines Nachlasses tätig. Sie kuratierte zahlreiche Gruppen- und Einzelausstellungen in Museen und Galerien weltweit, unter anderem zusammen mit Carles Guerra, Okwui Enwezor und Marius Babias. Ehmann ist zudem Mitherausgeberin mehrerer Bücher.

Harun Farocki (1944 Nový Jicín/CZ – Berlin/DE 2014) war ein in Berlin ansässiger Filmemacher, Medienkünstler und Theoretiker. Er studierte an der Deutschen Film- und Fernsehakademie Berlin. Sein Œuvre umfasst mehr als 120 Spielfilme, Essayfilme, Dokumentationen und Videoinstallationen. Farocki stellte in zahlreichen Gruppen- und Einzelausstellungen weltweit aus, nahm zweimal an der documenta (1997, 2007) sowie an der 56. Biennale von Venedig (2015) teil. Darüber hinaus hatte er Lehraufträge an der University of California in Berkeley (1993–99) und an der Akademie der bildenden Künste in Wien (2004–11).

Aldo Giannotti (1977 Genua/IT) lebt in Wien. Er studierte Video an der Accademia di Belle Arti di Carrara und Fotografie an der Akademie der Bildenden Künste München. Seine Arbeiten wurden in Zusammenarbeit mit verschiedenen Institutionen in Österreich geschaffen und präsentiert, u. a. der Albertina in

Wien, der Kunsthalle Wien, dem Lentos Museum in Linz, dem Kunsthaus Graz und vielen Institutionen im Ausland.

Liam Gillick (1964 Aylesbury/UK) lebt in New York. Er absolvierte das Hertfordshire College of Art und das Goldsmiths College der University of London. Neben seiner künstlerischen Tätigkeit arbeitet Gillick auch als Theoretiker, Kurator und Dozent. Er hat an zahlreichen wichtigen Ausstellungen teilgenommen, darunter an der documenta und den Biennalen in Venedig, Berlin und Istanbul. Er vertrat Deutschland bei der Biennale von Venedig 2009. Seine Arbeiten befinden sich in vielen öffentlichen Sammlungen, darunter im Centre Pompidou in Paris, im Guggenheim Museum in New York und Bilbao sowie im Museum of Modern Art in New York.

Lisa Großkopf (1989 Wien/AT) lebt in Wien. Sie studierte Grafikdesign sowie Fotografie und Mediendesign an der Kunstuniversität Linz, TransArts an der Universität für angewandte Kunst Wien und Kunst & Kommunikation an der Akademie der bildenden Künste Wien. Sie wurde mit dem Nachwuchsstipendium des österreichischen Bundeskanzleramtes, dem Gabriele-Heidecker-Preis und dem Fred-Adlmüller-Stipendium ausgezeichnet und war in Gruppen- und Einzelausstellungen in Österreich, Deutschland, der Slowakei, Norwegen, Israel und zahlreichen anderen Ländern vertreten.

Andreas Gursky (1955 Leipzig/DE) ist ein in Düsseldorf ansässiger Fotograf. Er studierte Visuelle Kommunikation an der Folkwang-Universität Essen und absolvierte seinen Master in Fotografie an der Kunstakademie Düsseldorf als Meisterschüler von Bernd und Hilla Becher. Seine Werke werden international ausgestellt und sind Teil zahlreicher Sammlungen, u. a. der Tate Modern, London, des Museums Ludwig, Köln, des Kunstmuseums Bonn, des Kunsthauses Zürich, des Kunstmuseums Basel oder des Metropolitan Museum of Art, New York.

Theresa Hattinger (1989 Salzburg/AT) ist Künstlerin und Designerin. Sie studierte Grafikdesign, Bühnenbild und Illustration an der Universität für angewandte Kunst in Wien, hat zahlreiche ortsspezifische Arbeiten im öffentlichen Raum gezeigt und an Bühnenbildern für experimentelle Stadterkundungsprojekte mitgearbeitet. Hattinger hat in Österreich, Deutschland, Kuba und Argentinien ausgestellt; ihre Arbeiten befinden sich in den Sammlungen des Museums für angewandte Kunst Wien, des Bundeslandes Salzburg und der Österreichischen Nationalbibliothek.

Michael Hieslmair (1974 Linz/AT) ist ein in Wien lebender Künstler, Architekt und Dozent. Er studierte Architektur an der Technischen Universität Graz und an der TU Delft. Seit 2005 arbeitet er mit Michael Zinganel an den Themen urbane und transnationale Mobilität, zeitgenössischer Massentourismus und Migration, z. B. für *Shrinking Cities* 2005, *Open Cities*, die 4. Internationale Architekturbiennale Rotterdam 2009 und Ruhr 2010, Kulturhauptstadt Europas. 2012 wurde er Mitbegründer des unabhängigen Forschungsinstituts Tracing Spaces und produzierte und kuratierte außerdem das Kunst-im-öffentlichen-Raum-Projekt *City on the Move – A Farewell to a Logistic Area* (mit Michael Zinganel).

Andreja Hribernik ist Kuratorin und seit 2023 Direktorin des Kunsthauses Graz. In ihrer Arbeit beschäftigt sie sich mit der komplexen Verflechtung von Museen als historische und geopolitische Räume, in denen zeitgenössische Kunst aktuelle Konflikte und Kämpfe hinterfragt und untersucht.

Tehching Hsieh (1950 Nan-Chou/TW) lebt in New York. In seinem Heimatland Taiwan begann er als Autodidakt zu malen, widmete sich aber bald ganz der Performance-Kunst. Seit der Jahrtausendwende, befreit von der Beschränkung, seine Werke während eines Zeitraums von dreizehn Jahren nicht zu zeigen, stellte Hsieh seine Arbeiten in Nord- und Südamerika, Asien und Europa aus. Schließlich wechselte er von der Produktion zur Veröffentlichung und Verbreitung von Kunst. Seine Ausstellung *Doing Time* wurde 2017 im taiwanesischen Pavillon auf der 57. Biennale von Venedig präsentiert, *One Year Performance 1980–1981* war 2017–2018 in der Tate Modern, London, und 2009 im MoMa und im Guggenheim Museum, New York, ausgestellt.

Katia Huemer ist Kuratorin der Ausstellung *24/7* und hat seit 2004 in verschiedenen Funktionen zahlreiche Ausstellungsprojekte, Veranstaltungen und Publikationen am Kunsthaus Graz realisiert. Sie ist Mutter, seit 2021 Mitglied des Green Teams des Universalmuseums Joanneum und mitverantwortlich für die Nachhaltigkeitsagenda des Kunsthauses. Aufgrund ihrer intensiven Beschäftigung mit dem Thema Arbeit ist sie seit 2024 auch Betriebsratsvorsitzende des Kunsthauses.

Johanna Kandl (1954 Wien/AT) lebt in Wien und Berlin. Sie studierte Konservierung und Restaurierung sowie Malerei an der Akademie der bildenden Künste in Wien sowie in Belgrad. Die Künstlerin wurde mit dem Niederösterreichischen Ehrenpreis in der Kategorie Bildende Kunst ausgezeichnet und hat vielfach im In- und Ausland ausgestellt. Sowohl allein als auch zusammen mit ihrem Mann Helmut Kandl hat sie in vielen Institutionen ihre Werke gezeigt, darunter im Kunsthaus Graz, im Lentos Kunstmuseum Linz, in der Kunsthalle Wien, in der Kunsthalle Basel und in der Kunsthalle Budapest.

Peter Kogler (1959 Innsbruck/AT) lebt in Wien. Er studierte an der Akademie der bildenden Künste in Wien und arbeitet seit den 1980er-Jahren als Medienkünstler mit Computergrafik, Film, Collage und Architektur. Er erhielt zahlreiche Auszeichnungen, darunter den Prix Ars Electronica (1988) und den Monsignore-Otto-Mauer-Preis (1988). Er hat national und international ausgestellt und mehrfach an der documenta und der Biennale von Venedig teilgenommen. Seit 1997 unterrichtete er als Professor an der Akademie der bildenden Künste Wien und seit 2008 an der Akademie der bildenden Künste München.

KURS wurde von zwei in Belgrad, Serbien, ansässigen Künstler*innen, Miloš Miletić und Mirjana Radovanović, gegründet. Gemeinsam widmen sie sich der bildenden Kunst und Forschung und untersuchen, wie künstlerische Praxis zu verschiedenen sozialen Themen beitragen und ein integraler Bestandteil davon werden kann. KURS hat in den letzten Jahren verschiedene Projekte realisiert, unter anderem das Forschungsprojekt *Lessons on Defense* (2016–2017) zur kulturellen Aktivität innerhalb der Volksbefreiungsbewegung, das Wandgemälde *Solidarity – to the International Brigades in Belgrade* und das Wandgemälde *Factory to the Workers* in der Itas-Prvomajska-Fabrik in Ivanec, Kroatien, im Rahmen des 13. Urban Festivals.

Silvio Lorusso (1985 Altamura/IT) ist ein in Lissabon ansässiger Schriftsteller, Künstler und Designer. Er erlangte einen MA in Visueller und Multimedia Kommunikation und ein Doktorat in Designwissenschaften von der Università Iuav di Venezia. Er ist Assistenzprofessor und Co-Direktor des Center for Other Worlds an der Lusófona University in Lissabon und Tutor am Institut für Informationsdesign an der Design Academy in Eindhoven. Seine Arbeiten waren unter anderem ausgestellt in: MaXXI, Rom, Transmediale, Berlin, The Photographers' Gallery, London, Kunsthalle Wien, NRW-Forum, Düsseldorf.

Agnes Maier ist seit 2015 fixer Bestandteil der österreichischen Poetry-Slam-Szene und auf nationalen und internationalen deutschsprachigen Bühnen zu Hause. Als Slam-Poetin ist sie mehrfache Landesmeisterin von Steiermark/Kärnten und gewann 2017 die österreichischen Staatsmeisterschaften im Team und im Einzel. 2020 gründete sie gemeinsam mit Christoph Steiner und Yannick Steinkellner das Slam Kollektiv Graz, mit dem sie Poetry Slams organisiert und moderiert. Sie arbeitet als freiberufliche Hebamme in Graz und ist Mutter einer Tochter, die 2008 zur Welt kam.

Luiza Margan (1983 Rijeka/HR) lebt in Wien. Sie studierte Malerei in Ljubljana und Performative Kunst und Skulptur an der Akademie der bildenden Künste in Wien. Ihre Arbeiten wurden in verschiedenen internationalen Institutionen und Galerien ausgestellt und sind Teil von Sammlungen wie der Generali Foundation in Salzburg, dem Belvedere 21 in Wien und dem MSU Zagreb.

Pia Mayrwöger (1986 Kefermarkt/AT) lebt in Linz. Sie studierte Experimentelles Design an der Kunstuniversität Linz. Ihre Arbeit wurde unter anderem mit dem

Arbeiterkammer Kunstpreis (2021), dem Arbeitsstipendium des Bundesministeriums für Bildung, Wissenschaft und Forschung (2021/2022) und dem Linz AG Atelierstipendium der Kunstförderpreise der Stadt Linz (2022/2023) ausgezeichnet. Sie präsentierte ihre Werke in Österreich und im Ausland, u. a. in Linz, Wien, Rotterdam und Riga.

Sam Meech (1981 Huddersfield/UK) lebt in Montreal, Kanada. Er studierte Multimediale Kunst an der Liverpool John Moores University und schloss ein Masters Degree an der Manchester Metropolitan University ab. Seine Arbeit vereint Projektionsdesign, interaktive Videoinstallationen, digitale Textilien und soziales Engagement. Er hat mehrere künstlerische Projekte für Organisationen wie FACT (Liverpool), The Lowry (Manchester), dem Open Data Institute (UK), dem Royal Opera House (UK), dem National Film Board of Canada, der Liverpool Biennial, dem British Film Institute und dem Staro Riga Festival entwickelt. Derzeit arbeitet er als Technischer Koordinator bei Vidéographe in Montreal.

Michail Michailov (1978 Veliko Tarnovo/BG) lebt in Wien und Paris. Er studierte Bildende Kunst an der Universität Veliko Tarnovo und schloss sein Studium der Kunstgeschichte an der Universität Wien ab. Michailov begann seine professionelle künstlerische Laufbahn in Österreich, wo er an mehreren Projekten in Zusammenarbeit mit der Künstlergruppe Gelitin teilnahm und an Einzel- und Gruppenkunstprojekten arbeitete. Michailov nahm an mehreren Residencies teil und stellte vielfach aus, hauptsächlich in Österreich, Bulgarien und Frankreich. 2022 vertrat er Bulgarien auf der 59. Biennale von Venedig.

Simon Nagy (1994 Wien/AT) ist ein in Wien ansässiger Künstler, Schriftsteller und Kulturvermittler. Er arbeitet in Zusammenhang mit verschiedenen Kollektiven in den Bereichen Kunst, Literatur und kritische Wissensproduktion. Nagy schreibt Essays, arbeitet zusammen mit jungen Menschen an queer-feministischen und geschichtspolitischen Themen, kreiert Filme, Ausstellungen und Lehrmaterial. Er ist Vorstandsmitglied von trafo.K, einem Büro für Kunstpädagogik und kritische Wissensproduktion, sowie Teil der Künstler*innengruppe Schandwache, Projektkoordinator des Kulturstudien- Forschungsprojekts *Saved Depth* am Institut für Germanistik an der Universität Wien und freischaffender Redakteur.

Marina Otero Verzier (1981 A Coruña/ES) ist Architektin und Forscherin. Sie studierte Architektur an der TU Delft und der ETSA Madrid, wo sie 2016 ihr Doktoratsstudium abschloss. 2013 erhielt sie als Fulbright Scholar ihren MS in Kritischen, Kuratorischen und Konzeptuellen Praktiken in der Architektur von der Graduate School of Architecture, Planning and Preservation der Columbia University. Otero ist in verschiedene unabhängige und institutionelle Forschungsinitiativen involviert. Derzeit unterrichtet sie an der Columbia University GSAPP, wo sie eine Forschungsinitiative mit Fokus auf dem Zusammenhang zwischen digitaler Infrastruktur und der Klimakatastrophe leitet. Ihre Arbeit wurde in verschiedenen Büchern und Journalen publiziert.

Elisa Giardina Papa (1979 Medicina/IT) lebt in New York und Sant' Ignazio in Sizilien. Sie studierte an der Politecnico in Mailand und der Rhode Island School of Design. Die Künstlerin hat in Film und Medien an der University of California, Berkeley promoviert und arbeitet als Assistant Professor of Modern Culture and Media an der Brown University. Ihre forschungsbasierten Arbeiten untersuchen Geschlechter, Sexualität und Arbeit im Verhältnis zu neoliberalem Kapitalismus und Technologie. Ihre Arbeiten wurden u. a. im MoMA in New York, im Unofficial Internet Pavillon der 54. Biennale di Venezia, im Haus der Elektronischen Künste (HeK) in Basel und in 319 Scholes in New York ausgestellt und aufgeführt.

Nika Radić (1968 Zagreb/HR) lebt in Berlin und Zagreb. Sie hat ein Studium in Skulptur an der Academy of Fine Arts in Zagreb sowie in Kunstgeschichte an der Universität Wien abgeschlossen. In ihren Videoarbeiten, Multimedia-Installationen und Fotografien konzentriert sie sich auf die Themen Kommunikation und die Art, wie Kunst Realität dokumentiert. Weiters schrieb sie über das Konzept der Subjektivität und ihre Texte wurden in internationalen Büchern und Zeitschriften publi-

ziert. Sie nahm an zahlreichen Einzel- und Gruppenausstellungen teil, u. a. in Zagreb, Berlin, Wien, Reykjavik und Mailand.

Katja Praznik ist Außerordentliche Professorin an der State University of New York in Buffalo und engagiert sich für die Entmystifizierung von Kunst als Arbeit, einschließlich der Organisation von Kunstschaffenden. Sie ist die Autorin von *Art Work: Invisible Labour and the Legacy of Yugoslav Socialism* (University of Toronto Press, 2021). Sie ist Mitbegründerin der Gewerkschaft Zasuk und Initiatorin von A Cultural Work Inspection. Ihre Arbeiten wurden in Zeitschriften wie *Historical Materialism* und *Social Text* sowie in zahlreichen Sammelbänden veröffentlicht, die sich mit Fragen der unbezahlten Arbeit in der Kunst befassen. Zuletzt in Praznik et al., *Which Side Are You On: Ideas for Reaching Fair Working Conditions in the Arts* (IETM, 2022).

Martha Rosler (1943 New York/US) lebt in New York. Sie studierte am Brooklyn College der City University of New York sowie an der University of California, San Diego. Ihre Arbeiten beinhalten Fotografie, Video, Installationen, Fotomontage und Performance. Rosler lehrte an verschiedenen Universitäten, hielt Workshops und Vorträge zu den Themen Fotografie, Medien und kritische Theorie. 2010 wurde der vielfach preisgekrönten Künstlerin der Guggenheim Museum Lifetime Achievement Award verliehen. Ihre Werke wurden in vielen verschiedenen Institutionen ausgestellt und sie hatte zahlreiche Einzelausstellungen, zuletzt in der Schirn Kunsthalle Frankfurt (2023), der Tate Modern in London (2022) und dem Museo de Arte Contemporáneo in Santiago (2019).

Sebastian Schmieg (1983 Tübingen/DE) lebt in Berlin. Er studierte an der Universität der Künste in Berlin (UdK). Schmieg arbeitet in einem breiten Spektrum von Medien, darunter Video, Website, Installation, Künstlerbuch, Costom Software und Lecture Performance. Seine Arbeiten wurden international ausgestellt, u. a. in der Kunsthalle Zürich, The Photographers' Gallery in London, im MdbK Leipzig, im HeK Basel und im Chronus Art Center in Shanghai. Er ist Professor für Interface Design an der HTW Dresden.

Christoph Schwarz (1981 Wien/AT) ist ein in Wien ansässiger Medienkünstler und Filmemacher. Er studierte Visuelle Medien und Digitale Kunst an der Universität für angewandte Kunst in Wien. Während er sich anfangs auf Videokunst, Installationen und Performances konzentrierte, widmete er sich mit der Zeit der Produktion von kurzen Spielfilmen. 2024 präsentierte das Festival des österreichischen Films Diagonale seinen ersten abendfüllenden Spielfilm, *Sparschwein*.

Selma Selman (1991 Ružica/BA) ist bildende Künstlerin und Aktivistin mit Romni-Wurzeln und lebt zwischen Bihać, Ružica, Amsterdam und New York. Nach ihrer Ausbildung in Malerei an der Fine Arts Academy in Banja Luka schloss Selman ihr MFA in Transmedia Visual and Performing Arts an der Syracuse University in New York ab. Sie ist Gründerin der Organisation Get The Heck To School, die Romni-Mädchen weltweit im Kampf gegen gesellschaftliche und armutsbedingte Ausgrenzung unterstützt. Ihre Werke wurden umfassend in Europa und den USA ausgestellt, unter anderem bei der documenta 15 und manifesta 14. Selmans Arbeiten sind Teil zahlreicher internationaler Sammlungen.

Santiago Sierra (1966 Madrid/ES) lebt in Madrid. Er studierte bildende Kunst an der Universidad Complutense in Madrid, der HFBK in Hamburg und der Academy of San Carlos in Mexiko City. Seine Arbeit umfasst eine weite Bandbreite von Medien, inklusive Installationen, Video, Performance und Fotografie. Er nahm an verschiedenen Gruppen- und Einzelausstellungen teil, unter anderem in der Tate Modern, London, dem KW Institute for Contemporary Art in Berlin, dem Palais de Tokyo in Paris, CAC in Malaga, im ICA in Boston und im P.S.1 Contemporary Art Center in New York und repräsentierte Spanien 2003 bei der 50. Biennale von Venedig.

Lia Sudermann (1985 Nürnberg/DE) lebt in Wien. Sie absolvierte die Kunsthochschule für Medien in Köln und studierte an der Akademie der bildenden Künste in Wien. Sie ist aktiv in den Bereichen Theater, Performance, Film und Video, Mitglied des Kunst- und Theaterkollektivs Postmodern Talking, (Co-)Autorin

und Performerin von Bühnenstücken und Lecture Performances. Sie hat ihre Arbeiten bei BEAST auf AEG in Nürnberg, der 47. Art Cologne 2013, der Nordbahn Halle in Wien sowie auf mehreren Filmfestivals präsentiert, inklusive den Job Film Days in Turin, dem Feminist Festival in Bucharest, REC.forward in Nizza und der Diagonale in Graz.

Eva Tropper ist seit 2022 Kuratorin für Fotografie an den Multimedialen Sammlungen, UMJ, und seit 2018 Teil des Leitungsteams der Museumsakademie Joanneum. Sie hat Geschichte, Romanistik und Medienkultur studiert und war in verschiedenen Projekten mit Schwerpunkt Visuelle Kultur an der Schnittstelle von Forschung und Museum tätig. Sie kuratierte für das GrazMuseum, das Photoinstitut Bonartes und das Pavelhaus/Pavlova Hiša und lehrte an den Universitäten Graz und Krems sowie am Masterstudienlehrgang für Visuelle Kultur der Universität Klagenfurt.

Oliver Walker (1980 Liverpool/UK) lebt in Berlin. Er studierte Bildende Kunst in Bristol und Art in Context an der Universität der Künste Berlin. Walker nahm an mehreren Residency-Programmen teil, zum Beispiel am Goethe Institut in Bangalore und BankArt 1929 in Yokohama. Seine Projekte wurden unter anderem in Berlin, Liverpool, Gdansk, Lund und Giorna präsentiert.

Michael Zinganel (1960 Bad Radkersburg/AT) ist Architekturtheoretiker, Kulturhistoriker, Kurator und Künstler mit Sitz in Wien. Er schloss sein Studium an der Fakultät für Architektur der Technischen Universität Graz ab, studierte Kunst an der Jan van Eyck Academy in Maastricht und promovierte in Zeitgeschichte an der Universität Wien. Er war Vorstandsmitglied und Kurator im Forum Stadtpark in Graz, Research Fellow am Internationalen Forschungszentrum Kulturwissenschaften (IFK) in Wien und lehrte an verschiedenen Universitäten und Akademien. Zinganel arbeitet intensiv an urbanen Themen, sowohl einzeln als auch in Kooperation mit anderen. Gemeinsam mit Michael Hieslmair gründete er 2012 die unabhängige Forschungsinstitution Trading Spaces.

Biographies

Maja Bajević (1967 Sarajevo/BA) lives in Paris. After classical training in former Yugoslavia, she studied at the École Nationale Supérieure des Beaux-Arts in Paris. In 2017 she was shortlisted for the Prix Marcel Duchamp. She has participated in numerous group and solo exhibitions, including the 56th Venice Biennale (2015) and documenta 12 in Kassel (2007), she has also exhibited in Ljubljana, Zurich, New York, Madrid, Berlin and Munich.

Julien Berthier (1975 Besançon/FR) lives in Paris. He attended the École Nationale Supérieure des Beaux-Arts in Paris and has been working internationally since the early 2000s. He aims to defy strict categorization, working across video, photography, sculpture, drawing and installation to create unusual but functional works that challenge our perspective. Berthier has participated in numerous group and solo exhibitions in France and abroad, including Vienna, Graz, Cologne, Brussels, Beijing and Los Angeles.

Louisa Clement (1987 Bonn/DE) lives in Bonn. She studied at Karlsruhe State Academy of Fine Arts and Düsseldorf Art Academy as a master-student of Andreas Gursky. The artist has exhibited in various institutions and museums in Germany and abroad. Her works are part of collections such as the Huis Marseille in Amsterdam, Atlanta Cultural Foundation in Bad Homburg, Collection of the City of Brühl and Ringier Collection in Zurich.

Manuel Correa (1991 Medellín/CO) is an artist and filmmaker. He studied Film and Media at Emily Carr University in Vancouver and completed his MA in Research Architecture at Goldsmiths College, University of London. His works have been presented in venues such as the Rotterdam International Film Festival, Museo Tamayo in Mexico, the 8th Norwegian Sculpture Biennial, Kunsternes Hus in Oslo and Het Nieuwe Instituut, amongst other spaces. He is currently working as part of the group Forensic Architecture.

Jeremy Deller (1966 London/UK) lives in London. He studied Art History at the Courtauld Institute and at the University of Sussex. He is an artist, curator and cultural activist known for his socially engaged and politically charged artwork. Deller was awarded the prestigious Turner Prize in 2004 and represented Great Britain at the 55th Venice Biennale in 2013. He has exhibited extensively worldwide, including Buenos Aires, Hong Kong, New York, Madrid, Paris and Tokyo.

Antje Ehmann (1968 Gelsenkirchen/DE) is a curator, author and artist based in Berlin. She collaborated with her life partner Harun Farocki for many years and currently works as custodian of his estate. She curated numerous group and solo exhibitions in museums and galleries worldwide, together with Carles Guerra, Okwui Enwezor, Marius Babias amongst others. Ehmann is co-editor of multiple books.

Harun Farocki (1944 Nový Jicín/CZ – Berlin/DE 2014) was a filmmaker, media artist and theorist, who lived and worked in Berlin. He studied at the German Film and Television Academy Berlin. His œuvre comprises more than 120 feature films, essay films, documentaries and video installations. Farocki had numerous group and solo exhibitions worldwide, he participated twice in documenta (1997, 2007) and at the 56th Venice Biennale (2015). He also held teaching positions at the University of California at Berkeley (1993–99) and at the Academy of Fine Arts in Vienna (2004–11).

Aldo Giannotti (1977 Genoa/IT) lives in Vienna. He studied at the Accademia di Belle Arti di Carrara in the field of video and at the Academy of Fine Arts in Munich in the field of photography. His work has been presented and created in collaboration with various institutions in Austria, including Albertina in Vienna, Kunsthalle Wien, Lentos Museum in Linz, Kunsthaus Graz and many institutions abroad.

Liam Gillick (1964 Aylesbury/UK) lives in New York. He graduated from Hertfordshire College of Art and Goldsmiths College of the University of London. In addition to his artistic work, Gillick also

works as a theorist, curator and educator. He has participated in numerous important exhibitions including documenta and the Venice, Berlin and Istanbul Biennales. He was representing Germany at Venice Biennale 2009. His work is held in many public collections including the Centre Pompidou in Paris, the Guggenheim Museum in New York and Bilbao and the Museum of Modern Art in New York.

Lisa Großkopf (1989 Vienna/AT) lives in Vienna. She studied Graphic Design and Photography and Media Design at the University of Art and Design Linz, TransArts at the University of Applied Arts Vienna and Art & Communication at the Academy of Fine Arts Vienna. She was awarded the grant for emerging artists by the Austrian Federal Chancellery, the Gabriele Heidecker Prize and the Fred Adlmüller grant. She has exhibited in group and solo exhibitions in Austria, Germany, Slovakia, Norway, Israel and numerous other countries.

Andreas Gursky (1955 Leipzig/DE) is a photographer based in Düsseldorf. He studied Visual Communication at Folkwang University in Essen and completed his master in Photography at the Academy of Art in Düsseldorf as a master-student of Bernd and Hilla Becher. His works are exhibited internationally and are part of many collections, including Tate Modern, London, Museum Ludwig, Cologne, Kunstmuseum Bonn, Kunsthaus Zürich, Kunstmuseum Basel, The Metropolitan Museum of Art, New York.

Theresa Hattinger (1989 Salzburg/AT) is an artist and designer. She studied Graphic Design, Stage Design and Illustration at the University of Applied Arts in Vienna. She has exhibited numerous site-specific works in public space and collaborated on stage designs for experimental urban exploration projects. She has exhibited in Austria, Germany, Cuba and Argentina; her work is represented in the collections of the Museum of Applied Arts Vienna, the Province of Salzburg and the Austrian National Library.

Michael Hieslmair (1974 Linz/AT) is an artist, architect and educator based in Vienna. He studied Architecture at Graz University of Technology and at Delft University of Technology. Since 2005 he has worked with Michael Zinganel on urban and transnational mobility, contemporary mass tourism and migration: e.g. for *Shrinking Cities* in 2005, *Open Cities*, the 4th International Architecture Biennale Rotterdam in 2009, at Ruhr 2010, European Capital of Culture. In 2012 he co-founded the independent research institute Tracing Spaces, also producing and curating the art in public space project *City on the Move – A Farewell to a Logistic Area* (with Michael Zinganel).

Andreja Hribernik is a curator and has been director of the Kunsthaus Graz since 2023. In her work, she addresses the issue of the complex intertwinement of museums as historcal and geopolitical spaces, where contemporary art questions and examines present conflicts and struggles.

Tehching Hsieh (1950 Nan-Chou/TW) lives in New York. He began painting as a self-taught artist in his home country of Taiwan, but soon devoted himself entirely to performance art. Since the millennium, Hsieh has exhibited his work in North and South America, Asia and Europe. He subsequently shifted from producing art to publicising and disseminating it. His exhibition *Doing Time* was presented by Taiwan Pavilion at 57th Venice Biennale 2017, *One Year Performance 1980–1981* was exhibited at Tate Modern, London, in 2017–2018, and MoMA and the Guggenheim Museum, New York, in 2009.

Katia Huemer is the curator of the exhibition *24/7* and has realised numerous exhibition projects, events and publications at the Kunsthaus Graz in various functions since 2004. She is mother, has been a member of the Universalmuseum Joanneum's Green Team since 2021 and is jointly responsible for the sustainability agenda at the Kunsthaus. Due to her intensive involvement with the topic of work, she has also been Chair of the Kunsthaus Works Council since 2024.

Johanna Kandl (1954 Vienna/AT) lives in Vienna and Berlin. She studied Conservation and Restoration and then Painting at the Academy of Fine Arts in Vienna, completed her studies in Belgrade. The

artist was awarded the Lower Austrian Honorary Prize in the category of Visual Art and has exhibited widely in Austria and abroad. She has exhibited solo and together with her husband Helmut Kandl in many institutions, including Kunsthaus Graz, Lentos Kunstmuseum Linz, Kunsthalle Wien, Kunsthalle Basel and Kunsthalle Budapest.

Peter Kogler (1959 Innsbruck/AT) lives in Vienna. He studied at the Academy of Fine Arts in Vienna and has been working as a media artist between computer graphics, film, collage and architecture since the 1980s. He has received numerous awards, such as the Prix Ars Electronica (1988) and the Monsignore Otto Mauer Prize (1988). He has exhibited nationally and internationally, participated multiple times in documenta and the Venice Biennale. He has been a Professsor at the Academy of Fine Arts in Vienna since 1979 and at the Academy of Fine Arts Munich since 2008.

KURS is formed by two artists, Miloš Miletić and Mirjana Radovanović, based in Belgrade, Serbia. They jointly practise visual art and research, exploring how artistic practice can contribute to and become an integral part of various social struggles. KURS has realised various projects in recent years, among others the research *Lessons on Defense* (2016–2017) on cultural activity within the People's Liberation Movement, the mural *Solidarity – to the International Brigades in Belgrade*, the mural *Factory to the Workers* at the Itas-Prvomajska factory in Ivanec, Croatia as part of the 13th Urban Festival.

Silvio Lorusso (1985 Altamura/IT) is a writer, artist and designer based in Lisbon. He received his MA in Visual and Multimedia Communications and holds a PhD in Design Sciences from the Iuav University of Venice. He is an Assistant Professor and co-director of the Center for Other Worlds at the Lusófona University in Lisbon and a tutor at the Information Design department of Design Academy Eindhoven. His work has been presented at, among other venues, MaXXI, Rome, Transmediale, Berlin, The Photographers' Gallery, London, Kunsthalle Wien, NRW-Forum, Düsseldorf.

Agnes Maier has been an established part of the Austrian poetry slam scene since 2015 and is present on national and international German-speaking stages. As a slam poet, she is a multiple national champion of Styria/Carinthia and won the Austrian national team and individual championships in 2017. In 2020, she founded the Slam Kollektiv Graz together with Christoph Steiner and Yannick Steinkellner, where she organises and moderates slams. She works as a freelance midwife in Graz and is the mother of a daughter who was born in 2008.

Luiza Margan (1983 Rijeka/HR) lives in Vienna. She studied Painting in Ljubljana and Performative Arts and Sculpture at the Academy of Fine Arts in Vienna. She has exhibited in numerous international institutional and gallery exhibitions. Her works are part of art collections like the Generali Foundation in Salzburg, Belvedere 21 in Vienna, or MSU Zagreb.

Pia Mayrwöger (1986 Kefermarkt/AT) lives in Linz. She studied Experimental Design at the Linz University of Art. Her work has been awarded, among others, with the Chamber of Labour Art Prize (2021), the Working Grant of the Federal Ministry for Education, Science and Research (2021/2022) and the Linz AG Studio Grant of the Art Promotion Prizes of the City of Linz (2022/2023). She has presented her work in Austria and abroad, including Linz, Vienna, Rotterdam and Riga.

Sam Meech (1981 Huddersfield/UK) is based in Montreal, Canada. He studied Multimedia Arts at Liverpool John Moores University and obtained an MA by Research at the Manchester Metropolitan University. His practice combines projection design, interactive video installation, digital textiles and community engagement. He has developed artistic commissions and projects for organisations including FACT (Liverpool), The Lowry (Manchester) Open Data Institute (UK), Royal Opera House (UK), National Film Board of Canada, Liverpool Biennial, British Film Institute, Staro Riga Festival. He currently works as a technical coordinator at Vidéographe in Montreal.

Michail Michailov (1978 Veliko Tarnovo/BG) lives in Vienna and Paris. He studied Fine Arts at the University of Veliko Tarnovo and completed his studies in Art History at the University of Vienna. He started his professional artistic career in Austria, taking part in several projects in cooperation with the artist group Gelitin and working on solo and group art projects. Michailov has participated in several residences and has exhibited extensively, mostly in Austria, Bulgaria and France. He represented Bulgaria at the 59th Venice Biennale in 2022.

Simon Nagy (1994 Vienna/AT) is an artist, writer and educator based in Vienna. He works in the context of various collectives in the fields of art, literature and critical knowledge production. He writes essays, collaborates with young people on queer feminist and historical-political topics and creates films, exhibitions and educational materials. He is a board member of trafo.K, an office for art education and critical knowledge production. He is part of the artist group Schandwache, a project collaborator in the cultural studies research project *Saved Depth* at the Institute for German Studies at the University of Vienna and a freelance editor.

Marina Otero Verzier (1981 A Coruña/ES) is an architect and researcher. She studied Architecture at TU Delft and the ETSA Madrid, where she completed her PhD in 2016. In 2013, as a Fulbright Scholar, she graduated with an MS in Critical, Curatorial and Conceptual Practices in Architecture from Columbia University's Graduate School of Architecture, Planning and Preservation. Otero is involved in various independent and institutional research initiatives. She currently teaches at Columbia University GSAPP where she is conducting a research initiative focused on the intersection between digital infrastructures and the climate catastrophe. Her work has been published in various books and journals.

Elisa Giardina Papa (1979 Medicina/IT) lives in New York and Sant' Ignazio in Sicily. She studied at Politecnico of Milan and Rhode Island School of Design. The artist holds a PhD in Film and Media from the University of California, Berkeley and works as an Assistant Professor of Modern Culture and Media at Brown University. Her research-based work investigates gender, sexuality and labour in relation to neoliberal capitalism and technology. Her work has been exhibited and screened at MoMA, New York, Unofficial Internet Pavilion of 54th Venice Biennale, Haus für elektronische Künste, Basel, 319 Scholes, New York, among others.

Katja Praznik is an Associate Professor at the State University of New York at Buffalo and committed to the demystification of art as labour, including organizing art workers. She is the author of *Art Work: Invisible Labour and the Legacy of Yugoslav Socialism* (University of Toronto Press, 2021). She is a co-founding member of the union Zasuk and initiator of A Cultural Work Inspection. Her work has been published in peer-reviewed journals from *Historical Materialism* to *Social Text*, and in many edited volumes dedicated to issues of unpaid labor in the arts. Most recently in: Praznik et al., *Which Side Are You On: Ideas for Reaching Fair Working Conditions in the Arts* (IETM, 2022).

Nika Radić (1968 Zagreb/HR) lives in Berlin and Zagreb. She holds a degree in Sculpture from the Academy of Fine Arts in Zagreb and in Art History from the University of Vienna. In her video works, multimedia installations and photographs she focuses on the subjects of communication and the ways art documents reality. She has also written on the idea of subjectivity, and her texts were published in books and magazines internationally. She has participated in numerous solo and group shows, in Zagreb, Berlin, Vienna, Reykjavik and Milan, among others.

Martha Rosler (1943 New York/US) lives in New York. She studied at Brooklyn College of the City University of New York and the University of California, San Diego. Her work encompasses photography, video, installation, photomontage and performance. She has taught at various universities, held workshops and lectured widely on photography, media and critical theory. She received the

Guggenheim Museum Lifetime Achievement Award in 2010 and many other awards. She has exhibited widely at various institutions, with numerous solo exhibitions, recently at the Schirn Kunsthalle Frankfurt (2023), Tate Modern, London (2022) and Museo de Arte Contemporáneo, Santiago (2019).

Sebastian Schmieg (1983 Tübingen/DE) lives in Berlin. He studied at the Berlin University of the Arts (UdK). Schmieg works in a wide range of media, including video, website, installation, artist book, custom software and lecture performance. His work has been exhibited internationally at, among others, Kunsthalle Zurich, The Photographers' Gallery London, MdbK Leipzig, HeK Basel, and Chronus Art Center Shanghai. He is a professor for interface design at HTW Dresden.

Christoph Schwarz (1981 Vienna/AT) is a media artist and filmmaker who lives in Vienna. He studied Visual Media and Digital Art at the University of Applied Arts Vienna. Initially focusing on video art, installations and performances, over time he dedicated himself to the production of short feature films. In 2024, the Austrian film festival Diagonale presented its first feature-length film, *Sparschwein*.

Selma Selman (1991 Ružica/BA) is a visual artist and activist of Romani origin, who lives between Bihać, Ružica, Amsterdam and New York. Following her education in Painting at the Fine Arts Academy in Banja Luka, Selman completed her MFA in Transmedia Visual and Performing Arts at Syracuse University in New York. She is the founder of the organisation Get The Heck To School, which aims to empower Romani girls all around the world who face ostracisation from society and poverty. She has exhibited extensively across Europe and the United States, including documenta 15 and manifesta 14. Her work is part of numerous international collections.

Santiago Sierra (1966 Madrid/ES) lives in Madrid. He studied Fine Arts at the Universidad Complutense in Madrid, the HFBK in Hamburg and at the Academy of San Carlos in Mexico City. His work spans a variety of mediums, including installation, video, performance and photography. He has participated in numerous group and solo exhibitions, among others at Tate Modern, London, KW Institute for Contemporary Art, Berlin, Palais de Tokyo, Paris, CAC, Malaga, ICA, Boston, and P.S.1 Contemporary Art Center, New York. He represented Spain at the 50th Venice Biennale in 2003.

Lia Sudermann (1985 Nuremberg/DE) lives in Vienna. She graduated from the Academy of Media Arts in Cologne and completed Critical Studies at the Academy of Fine Arts in Vienna. She is active in the areas of theatre, performance, film and video. She is a member of the art and performance collective Postmodern Talking, (co-)author and performer of stage plays and lecture performances. She has presented her work at the BEAST auf AEG in Nuremberg, the 47th Art Cologne 2013, the Nordbahn Halle in Vienna and several film festivals, including Job Film Days in Turin, Feminist Film Festival in Bucharest, REC.forward in Nice and Diagonale in Graz.

Eva Tropper has been Curator of Photography at the Multimedia Collections (Universalmuseum Joanneum) since 2022 and part of the management team of the Joanneum Museum Academy since 2018. She studied History, Romance Studies and Media Culture and has worked on various projects focussing on visual culture at the interface between research and museums. She has curated for the GrazMuseum, the Photoinstitut Bonartes and the Pavelhaus/Pavlova Hiša and taught at the Universities of Graz and Krems as well as on the Master's Programme for Visual Culture at the University of Klagenfurt.

Oliver Walker (1980 Liverpool/UK) lives in Berlin. He studied Fine Art in Bristol and Art in Context at the University of the Arts in Berlin. He has participated in several residency programs, including Goethe Institute in Bangalore and BankArt1929 in Yokohama. His projects have been presented in Liverpool, Berlin, Gdansk, Lund and Girona, among others.

Michael Zinganel (1960 Bad Radkersburg/AT) is an architecture theorist, cultural historian, curator and artist based in Vienna. He graduated at the Faculty of Architecture at Graz University of Technology, studied art at the Jan van Eyck Academy in Maastricht and obtained a PhD in Contemporary History at the University of Vienna. Zinganel had been a board member and curator at Forum Stadtpark in Graz, a research fellow at the IFK (International Centre for Cultural Studies) in Vienna and taught at various universities and academies. He works intensively on urban issues, solo and in cooperation. Together with Michael Hieslmair he co-founded the independent research institute Tracing Spaces in 2012.

Dank an Thanks to

Mustafa Ali
Farzana Haqjo
Adrian Heathfield
Gerald Kuhn (ISOP)
Pia Razenberger
Stefan Tiefengraber

Eva Tropper, Astrid Aschacher
(Museum für Geschichte)

Jooyoung Friedman-Buchanan (EAI)
Ellie Royle, Laura Plant, Charlotte Rusk (THE MODERN INSTITUTE/TOBY WEBSTER LTD.)

Gabriella Kolandra
(Studio Elisa Giardina Papa)
Julian Moeller (Studio Peter Kogler)
Tamika Odhiambo, Iva Vukic
(Studio Selma Selman)
Manuela Otero, Hella Spinelli
(Estudio Santiago Sierra)
Annette Völker (Atelier Gursky)

Alexandra Cravignac, Dorian Dogaru
(Galerie Vallois)
Meike Denker (Kunst & Denker)
Isabelle Erben
(Galerie Nagel Draxler GmbH)
Désirée Gross, Annemarie Reichen
(Galerie Peter Kilchmann)
Róna Kopeczky (acb gallery)
Li Tasser (MEYER*KAINER)

Den Künstler*innen der Ausstellung gilt unser größter Dank. Es war wunderbar, mit euch zu ARBEITEN!
Our warmest thanks go to the artists of the exhibition. It was wonderful to WORK with you!

Diese Publikation erscheint anlässlich der Ausstellung / This catalogue was published for the exhibition

24/7
Arbeit zwischen Sinnstiftung und Entgrenzung
Work between meaning and imbalance
01.05.2024–19.01.2025

Kunsthaus
Graz

Direktorin / Director:
Andreja Hribernik

Die Kunsthaus Graz GmbH steht je zur Hälfte im Eigentum der Stadt Graz und der Universalmuseum Joanneum GmbH, einer Gesellschaft des Landes Steiermark. / Kunsthaus Graz GmbH is equally owned by the City of Graz and the Universalmuseum Joanneum GmbH, a company of the Province of Styria.

Ausstellungsteam Exhibition team

Kuratorin / Curator: Katia Huemer
Assistenzkurator / Assistant curator: Martin Grabner
Registratur / Registrar: Magdalena Muner
Ausstellungsarchitektur / Exhibition architecture: studio itzo: Rainer Stadlbauer, Martina Schiller, Yoko Halbwidl
Grafische Gestaltung / Graphic design: Đorđe Balmazović
Grafische Umsetzung / Graphic realisation: Karin Buol-Wischenau
Übersetzungen / Translations: Kate Howlett-Jones
Konservierung, Restaurierung / Conservation, restoration: Mariia Bakhareva, Paul-Bernhard Eipper, Tanja Gasser
Ausstellungsaufbau / Exhibition construction: DO-DESIGN: Daniel Oberthaler, Felix Dokonal, Janosch Webersink; Johannes Herster, Leon Podesser; Gordon Sherriff
Elektrik, Licht / Electricity, light: Peter Rumpf, Sebastian Schumacher
Malerarbeiten / Paintwork: Peter Koren, Georg Sperl
Vorproduktion / Pre-production: Robert Bodlos und / and Team
Tapezierarbeiten / Wallpaper work: Rainer Werbearchitektur: Hannes Rainer
Reinigung / Cleaning: Michaela Hofmann, Aziz Tadrous, Marija Vuckovic
Kunstvermittlung / Art education: Monika Holzer-Kernbichler und / and Team

Mit freundlicher Unterstützung von / Kindly supported by

powered by

österreichische LOTTERIEN UNIQA

Committed to the UN Sustainable Development Goals

4 HOCHWERTIGE BILDUNG · 5 GESCHLECHTER-GLEICHHEIT · 8 MENSCHENWÜRDIGE ARBEIT UND WIRTSCHAFTS-WACHSTUM · 10 WENIGER UNGLEICHHEITEN

In Kooperation mit Museum für Geschichte / In cooperation with History Museum: *Alles Arbeit / It's All Work*

Kunsthaus Graz
Lendkai 1
8020 Graz, Austria
T +43 316 8017 9200
info@kunsthausgraz.at
www.kunsthausgraz.at

Katalogteam Catalogue team

Herausgeberinnen / Editors-in-chief:
Katia Huemer, Andreja Hribernik
Katalogredaktion / Editors:
Martin Grabner, Katia Huemer
Autor*innen / Authors:
Martin Grabner, Katia Huemer, Agnes Maier, Simon Nagy, Katja Praznik, Eva Tropper
Werktexte / Work texts:
Katia Huemer, Martin Grabner
Glossar / Glossary: Katia Huemer
Biografien / Biographies:
Aleksandra Żelichowska
Lektorat deutsch / German proofreading:
Jörg Eipper-Kaiser
Lektorat englisch / English proofreading:
Kate Howlett-Jones, Karin Buol-Wischenau
Übersetzung Deutsch-Englisch / Translations German-English: Kate Howlett-Jones, Teresa Faudon, Christopher Hütmannsberger, Miriam Stoney
Übersetzung Englisch-Deutsch / Translation English-German: Teresa Faudon
Grafische Gestaltung / Graphic design:
Karin Buol-Wischenau
Druck / Print: Print Alliance, Bad Vöslau
Print Alliance HAV Produktions GmbH, 2540 Bad Vöslau
Papier / Paper:
Vivus 89, 80 g/m², Arctic Volume 115 g/m²

Gedruckt in Österreich. / Printed in Austria.

Produziert nach den Richtlinien des Österreichischen Umweltzeichens
Produced in accordance with the guidelines of the Austrian Ecolabel

UW-Nr. 715

Druckprodukt mit finanziellem Klimabeitrag
ClimatePartner.com/13996-2406-1072

ISBN 978-3-99153-135-7

Erschienen im / Published by:
VfmK Verlag für moderne Kunst GmbH
Schwedenplatz 2/24
A-1010 Wien / Vienna
hello@vfmk.org
www.vfmk.org

Vertrieb / Distribution:
Europa / Europe: LKG, www.lkg-va.de
Worldwide: D.A.P., www.artbook.com

Bibliografische Information der Deutschen Nationalbibliothek
Die Deutsche Nationalbibliothek verzeichnet diese Publikation in der Deutschen Nationalbibliografie; detaillierte bibliografische Daten sind im Internet über dnb.de abrufbar. / Bibliographic information published by the Deutsche Nationalbibliothek
The Deutsche Nationalbibliothek lists this publication in the Deutsche Nationalbibliografie; detailed bibliographic data is available in the Internet at dnb.de

Fotocredits Photo credits

S. / p. 4: Foto / Photo: Sebastian Schaub, © Bildrecht, Wien 2024
S. / p. 5: © Bildrecht, Wien 2024
S. / pp. 6/7: Foto / Photo: Aurélien Mole, © Bildrecht, Wien 2024
S. / p. 9: © Luisa Clement & Cassina Projects Milan
S. / pp. 10, 11: © Manuel Correa, Marina Otero Verzier
S. / p. 13: Foto / Photo: Cristiano Corte, © Jeremy Deller
S. / p. 14: © Nojus Drąsutis, Courtesy Antje Ehmann / Harun Farocki GbR
S. / p. 15: © Gladys Lizarazu, Courtesy Antje Ehmann / Harun Farocki GbR
S. / pp. 18, 19: © Harun Farocki GbR
S. / p. 21: © Bildrecht, Wien 2024
S. / pp. 22/23: Pinacoteca Agnelli, Turin, 2022, Foto / Photo: Andrea Guermani, © Bildrecht, Wien 2024
S. / pp. 24, 25: Foto / Photo: Lisa Großkopf, © Bildrecht, Wien 2024
S. / pp. 26/27: Courtesy Sprüth Magers, © Andreas Gursky / Bildrecht, Wien 2024
S. / p. 29: Projekt Cargo Vienna, 2023, Foto / Photo: Christopher Mavric, © Tracing Spaces (Hattinger/Hieslmair/Zinganel) & Bildrecht, Wien 2024
S. / p. 31: Foto / Photo: Michael Shen, © Tehching Hsieh
S. / pp. 32, 33: © Johanna Kandl
S. / p. 34: documenta IX, Museum Fridericanum Kassel, 1992, Foto / Photo: Dirk Pauwels, © Peter Kogler
S. / p. 35: © Peter Kogler
S. / pp. 36, 37: © KURS (Mirjana Radovanović, Miloš Miletić)
S. / pp. 38/39: © Silvio Lorusso
S. / pp. 40, 41: © Luiza Margan & Bildrecht, Wien 2024
S. / p. 43: Foto / Photo: Theresa Muhl, © Bildrecht, Wien 2024
S. / pp. 44, 45: © Sam Meech
S. / pp. 46, 47: © Michail Michailov & Bildrecht, Wien 2024
S. / pp. 48, 49: © Elisa Giardina Papa
S. / p. 51: © Nika Radić & Bildrecht, Wien 2024
S. / pp. 52, 53: © Martha Rosler, Electronic Arts Intermix (EAI), New York & Galerie Nagel Draxler Berlin/Köln/München
S. / pp. 54, 55: © Sebastian Schmieg & Silvio Lorusso
S. / pp. 56, 57: © Christoph Schwarz
S. / pp. 58, 59: Foto / Photo: Tibor Varga Somogyi, © Selma Selman & acb gallery
S. / pp. 60, 61: ACVIC Barcelona, 2022, © Santiago Sierra & Bildrecht, Wien 2024
S. / pp. 62, 63: © Lia Sudermann & Simon Nagy
S. / pp. 64, 65: © Oliver Walker
S. / p. 67: Nojus Drąsutis, *The Pool Cleaners, Vilnius 2017*, aus / from: Antje Ehmann, Harun Farocki, *Eine Einstellung zur Arbeit / Labour in a Single Shot*, 2011–2021
S. / pp. 70–73, 78/79, 86–89, 97, 103, 109, 116–125, 137, 142/143, 148–151, 161–169, 182–185, 190/191, 202/203, 210: Martin Grabner/Kunsthaus Graz
S. / pp. 76/77, 90/91, 132, 141, 146/147, 194, 196/197: N. Lackner/UMJ
S. / p. 104: Reithofer Media/Simon Reithofer
S. / pp. 112/113: Katia Huemer, Martin Grabner, Nadine Kröpfl, N. Lackner, Claus Sondergelt, studio-lou.at/Lukas Elsneg u. a. / a. o.
S. / pp. 126/127, 144/145, 208/209: Janosch Foto.Film | Janosch Webersink
S. / p. 155: Courtesy Apparatus 22
S. / pp. 170/171, 178: studio-lou.at/ Lukas Elsneg
S. / p. 175: Courtesy Apparatus 22, Foto / Photo: Anne Faucheret

Künstler*innen vertreten von / Artists represented by Bildrecht, Wien 2024: Maja Bajević, Julien Berthier, Aldo Giannotti, Liam Gillick, Lisa Großkopf, Andreas Gursky, Luiza Margan, Pia Mayrwöger, Michail Michailov, Nika Radić, Santiago Sierra, Michael Zinganel